WALKER PERCY
AND THE
POSTMODERN WORLD

WALKER PERCY
AND THE
POSTMODERN WORLD

Mary K. Sweeny

LOYOLA UNIVERSITY PRESS

Loyola University Press
3441 North Ashland Avenue
Chicago, IL 60657

Design by C. L. Tornatore
Illustrations by Arist Kirsch

Grateful acknowledgment is given to the following publishers:

Excerpts from *The Last Gentleman* by Walker Percy. Copyright © 1966 by Walker
Percy. Reprinted by permission of Farrar, Straus and Giroux, Inc. Excerpts from
Love in the Ruins by Walker Percy. Copyright © 1971 by Walker Percy. Reprinted
by permission of Farrar, Straus and Giroux, Inc. Excerpts from *The Message in the
Bottle* by Walker Percy. Copyright © 1954, 1956, 1957, 1958, 1959, 1961, 1967, 1975
by Walker Percy. Reprinted by permission of Farrar, Straus and Giroux, Inc.
Excerpts from *Lancelot* by Walker Percy. Copyright © 1977 by Walker Percy.
Reprinted by permission of Farrar, Straus and Giroux, Inc. Excerpts from *The
Second Coming* by Walker Percy. Copyright © 1980 by Walker Percy. Reprinted by
permission of Farrar, Straus and Giroux, Inc.

Excerpt from *The Phenomenon of Man* by Pierre Teilhard de Chardin. Reprinted
by permission of Harper and Row Publishers, Inc., copyright © 1957.

Excerpts from *The Moviegoer* by Walker Percy. Copyright © 1961 by Alfred A.
Knopf, Inc.

Excerpts from *The End of the Modern World* by Romano Guardini. Used with
permission of Sheed & Ward, Kansas City, Mo. 64141.

Excerpt from *Monsignor Quixote* by Graham Greene. Used with permission of
Simon and Schuster, copyright © 1982.

Library of Congress Cataloging-in-Publication Data

Sweeny, Mark K.
    Walker Percy and the postmodern world.

    (A Campion book)
    Bibliography: p. 81
    Includes index.
    1. Percy, Walker, 1916-   —Criticism and
interpretation.   2. Percy, Walker, 1916-
—Philosophy.   I. Title.
PS3566.E6912Z835   1987   813′ .54   86-27474
ISBN 0-8294-0541-0

For Walker Percy

Gadfly, born to search for a host.
Orphan spawned of warm winds, sun and swamp mist
Blown north to wander in city crevasse and fetid air,
There disoriented, finding nothing.
He traced circles backward on a reach for life.
Lost, alone, with a hunger larger than himself
He wandered, a castaway, among scrub oak and hummock,
With his thousand, thousand eyes, searched for life.
Drawn by hawk's circle, saw,
Found his willing Host waiting.
He spiralled with glazed wing and open spear
To sting: eat and drink flesh and blood,
The bread of his longing and the wine of his joy.
Spinning up in dizzied rapture and spilling his song,
Again to cling and taste again
New in his joy, new in his home—
Gadfly. Godfly.

CONTENTS

ACKNOWLEDGMENTS

Without the inspiration and support of my thesis advisor, Dr. David M. LaGuardia of John Carroll University, and the loving encouragement and understanding of my husband, John, and our son, Paul, and our daughter, Mary Sweeny Hornung, this study would never have come to fruition. I am deeply grateful to them and all the others who helped these seeds sprout and grow.

INTRODUCTION

In his novels Walker Percy presents his view of modern man lost to himself in the categories in which science and technology have placed him. He is mass man, unable to act personally in the everyday world unless he is directed by the "experts." He is a castaway on the island of life looking for a message in a bottle. Percy has said in an interview that "what I name is the Judeo-Christian view of man in trouble, as the sparks fly up, which is the way man is. The thing I am concerned with is the peculiar predicament of late twentieth-century man, and especially in the American South" (Linda W. Hobson, "The Study of Consciousness: An Interview with Walker Percy," *Georgia Review,* 35 [Spring 1981] 53).

What concerns Percy is the portrait of modern existential man at home anywhere and nowhere, a portrait also presented by such other probing novelists as John Updike, Saul Bellow, and Graham Greene; and earlier, by Hemingway, Camus, and Sartre. But Percy's portrait incorporates Søren Kierkegaard's necessary leap to faith and Gabriel Marcel's added dimension of love. His view is a Christian existential view.

While Walker Percy is also noted as a philosopher, having published in 1975 a collection of philosophical essays, *The Message in the Bottle*, the focus for this study will be on his five novels: *The Moviegoer* (1961), *The Last Gentleman* (1966), *Love in the Ruins* (1971), *Lancelot* (1977), and *The Second Coming* (1980). As the philosophical ideas surface as part of his fiction's themes, they will be considered.

Percy depicts modern man in a state of extraordinary fragmentation as a result of living in a world that has lost its bearings and is disintegrating. Referring to the end of the modern world, he writes about it in the hope of helping to prevent a calamity, but he does not claim to have been given a vision of the future. His hypothesis is based on the present condition of man. In his essay, "Notes for a Novel about the End of the World," Percy declares: "The novelist is less like a prophet than he is like the canary that coal miners used to take down into the shaft to test the air. When the canary gets unhappy, utters plaintive cries, and collapses, it may be time for the miners to surface and think things over" (Walker Percy, *The Message in the Bottle* [New York: Farrar, Straus and Giroux, 1975] 101).

To Percy, the serious novelist is like "a man teetering on the brink of the abyss here and now, or worse, like a man who is already over the brink and into the

abyss ... " quite apart from the threat of nuclear cataclysm (Percy, *Message*, 102). The protagonists of his
novels are all like that, teetering; yet they continure to
search for meaning. This study argues that Percy's protagonists pass from awareness of their malaise, to a
search and journey, to belief and communion with
other individuals in the same process.

Percy defines the novelist as "a writer who has an
explicit and ultimate concern with the nature of man
and the nature of reality where man finds himself" (Percy, *Message*, 102). In this concern he joins an increasing
number of thinkers, including Romano Guardini, Pope
John Paul II, R. Buckminster Fuller and E.F. Schumacher,
whose works have helped to inspire antinuclear disar-
mament groups, environmentalists, survivalists, and
millenarians. Percy himself sees the predicament of the
individual man in a technological world, but instead of
condemning technology, he underscores man's use of it.

Attracted to the "beauties of the scientific method," he trained as a physician, but early in his medical
profession, he contracted tuberculosis. While recover-
ing, he turned to philosophy in his own personal search
and eventually began writing: first, philosophical essays
and later, novels, all of which show his awareness that
science does not concern itself with the individual but
only with the individual as part of a group. In fact, he
says, the individual is lost in the scientific concept of
Mass Man.

R. Buckminster Fuller, inventor-physicist-designer-
thinker, has both reveled in the great accomplishments
of technology and warned of dangers in its application.
In his last work, *Critical Path*, Fuller places his hope for
the future with the individual man, and addresses each
individual urgently "because of my driving conviction

that all of humanity is in peril of extinction if each one of us does not dare, now and henceforth, always to tell only the truth, and all the truth and to do so promptly—right now." He cites the failure of organizations, whether political, religious, economic or social, to represent the many, and places his faith only in the "intuitive wisdom of the individual to avert catastrophe. Technology has advanced to a point where there are enough resources to sustain our world indefinitely, if used properly, or to destroy it" (R. Buckminster Fuller, *The Critical Path* [New York: St. Martin's Press, 1981] xi).

Similarly, in his essay entitled "Notes for a Novel about the End of the World," Percy avers that the novelist:

> finds—in himself and in other people—a new breed of person in whom the potential for catastrophe—and hope—has suddenly escalated. Everyone knows about the awesome new weapons. But what is less apparent is a comparable realignment of energies within the human psyche. The psychical forces presently released in the postmodern consciousness open unlimited possibilities for both destruction and liberation, for an absolute loneliness or a rediscovery of community and reconciliation (*Message*, 112).

The disquieted canary, the modern novelist, must be concerned with even deeper issues than those of the nuclear bomb, racism, and Vietnam. According to Percy's definition, a novelist is obliged to be "religious" in the sense of "signifying a radical bond" that is important to man's connection with reality. He includes in his list of writers who are so concerned: Dostoevsky, Tolstoy, Camus, Sartre, Faulkner, and Flannery O'Connor.

In citing Sartre, he comments, "Sartre, one might object, is an atheist. He is, but his atheism is 'religious' in the sense intended here: that the novelist betrays a passionate conviction about man's nature, the world, and man's obligation in the world" (Percy, *Message*, 103). Whereas the Russian writers, such as Tolstoy and Dostoevsky, were "haunted by God," many of the French existentialists are "haunted by his absence."

The same "religious" concern manifests itself in the often violent, shocking novels of today, Percy adds. The modern novelist's view is apt to be widely divergent from the views of the leaders of the secular city, and "in particular from the views of the new theologians of the secular city" (*Message*, 104). He is able to sense, more than that theologian, who has for years asserted his friendship with the advances of science and technology, the discrepancies in this melding. The modern novelist may shock his readers when he speaks of last things, Percy asserts, "if not the Last Day of the Gospels, then of a possible coming destruction, of a laying waste of cities, of vineyards reverting to the wilderness" (*Message,* 104).

Percy poses this question: "Is it too much to say that the novelist, unlike the new theologian, is one of the few remaining witnesses to the doctrine of original sin, the imminence of catastrophe in paradise?" (*Message,* 106). He adds that "It is the novelist who, despite his well-advertised penchant for violence, his fetish for freedom, his sexual adventurism, pronounces anathemas upon the most permissive of societies, which in fact permits him everything" (*Message*, 110). It seems, nonetheless, that the successful American novelist, who is enjoying status and financial benefits heretofore unknown in the literary world, suffers a profound disquiet, whether he be Christian, atheist, Jew.

Speaking of Christian novelists in particular, a group of which he is a part, Percy states: "I do not conceive it my vocation to preach the Christian faith in a novel, but as it happens, my world view is informed by a certain belief about man's nature and destiny which cannot fail to be central to any novel I write." Among the advantages of this is to see man "as by his very nature an exile and wanderer rather than as a behaviorist sees him: as an organism in an environment." He contends that Camus fits into this idea, in spite of his break with Christianity; Percy discovers in Camus's stranger "blood ties with the wayfarer of Saint Thomas Aquinas and Gabriel Marcel. And if it is true that we are living in eschatological times, times of enormous danger and commensurate hope, of possible end and possible renewal, the prophetic-eschatological character of Christianity is no doubt peculiarly apposite" (*Message*, 111).

A hope can be found in the writings of Buckminster Fuller, but his hope is not based on Christianity. Fuller sees in the Western world what Percy calls the "massive failure of Christendom itself" (*Message*, 111). But Percy does not perceive this failure in the same sense as the scientific humanist, who regards Christianity as an anachronism. Rather, Percy makes a distinction when he indicts "Christendom" and not Christianity or Christ and His "Good News." He implies that in the mass acceptance and universal following of present-day Christian congregations, we witness a majority which believes in Christianity and takes it for granted to the point where its essence is largely ignored. In the South, Percy implies, the Christian sects have been largely politicized. He satirizes this notion in several of his novels, notably *Love in the Ruins* and *The Second Coming*.

Somehow Percy finds hope in this devastation of the psyche where few other novelists have yet to find it. He discovers uncontaminated air in our poisonous, adulterated cloud of ideas. While many modern thinkers come to the end of meaning, finding only emptiness, Percy sees old pretenses falling away and speaks about a new consciousness. The "canary" will emerge from the mining shaft to the purified air of belief.

The influence of existentialists like Sartre, Camus, Marcel, and especially Kierkegaard upon Percy's novels and philosophical essays has been discussed in detail by Robert Coles in his book, *Walker Percy: An American Search,* and by Martin Luschei in *The Sovereign Wayfarer*; however, an even more important influence is that of Romano Guardini, theologian and philosopher. Although Coles and Luschei barely mention Guardini, Percy quotes significantly from Guardini's little book *The End of the Modern World* in *The Last Gentleman*; and in *Love in the Ruins* Percy echoes the stark split at the end of the modern world described by Guardini and takes us into the "terrible loneliness" in faith of the postmodern era which Guardini has delineated before him. Guardini states:

> We know now that the modern world is coming to an end.... At the same time, the unbeliever will emerge from the fogs of secularism. He will cease to reap benefit from the values and forces developed by the very Revelation he denies.... Loneliness in faith will be terrible. Love will disappear from the face of the public world, but the more precious will be that love which flows from one lonely person to another ... the world to come will be filled with animosity and danger, but it will be a world open and clean (Romano Guardini, *The End*

of the Modern World [New York: Sheed and Ward, 1956] 132-33).

This is the eschatological world that Percy and Guardini each have envisioned—a more honest world where words will mean what they connote, where the choices may be stark but obvious, where ultimate concerns will be accepted or rejected, where the few with genuine love and faith may have to stand alone. But with these few will rest the hope of renewal, the hope of saving the gift of a habitable planet from complete destruction.

In other sections of his book, Guardini, like Walker Percy in his essays and novels, traces in the modern era the reasons for the loss of man's individuality and his hold on reality.

Guardini further elaborates on his vision of the future which contains along with the Fall, the hope of progress to "sense the mystery of the final *why?*" Guardini's hope includes the possibility that:

> perhaps love will achieve an intimacy and harmony never known to this day. Perhaps it will gain what lies hidden in the key words of the providential message of Jesus (Matthew 6:33): that things are transformed for the man who makes God's Will for His Kingdom his first concern (*End*, 132).

Guardini does not talk of an end in the sense of time, but:

> nearness as it pertains to the essence of the End, for in essence man's existence is now nearing an absolute decision. Each and every consequence of that decision bears with it the greatest potentiality and the most extreme danger (*End*, 133).

Pierre Teilhard de Chardin envisions a similar future in *The Phenomenon of Man*:

> Either nature is closed to our demands for futurity, in which case thought, the fruit of millions of years of effort, is stifled, still-born in a self-abortive and absurd universe. Or else an opening exists—that of the super-soul above our souls; but in that case the way out, if we are to agree to embark on it, must open out freely onto limitless psychic spaces in a universe to which we can unhesitatingly entrust ourselves (New York: Harper and Row, 1959, 231-32).

Both Guardini and Teilhard de Chardin were priests and theologians, and both base their hopes for the future upon God as their center. Guardini constructs his treatise from a historical overview, while Teilhard fashions his by examining the evolution of the universe, but they are in agreement about the end of "modern man" in this age and the beginning of a new era where man regains individual sovereignty.

We discover these two threads woven into Walker Percy's call for a new consciousness, based upon an individual's regaining of his own sovereignty in opposition to the dictates of behavioristic psychology. Recovery of sovereignty is the struggle of the protagonists of his novels, the point of his philosophical essays, his hope of the future in the new age before which we stand. Sovereignty of the individual and a resultant new consciousness are the points that find simultaneous agreement from his fellow thinkers: Fuller, Teilhard de Chardin, Guardini, and others. The trumpet sounds, muffled as if from underwater. In the twittering protest of the canary in the mine, the note entoned is one of individual thought, individual responsibility amidst the equalizing objectivity of science, the dull gray straight lines of mass society, and the creative, progressive deviations or variations of the one, the individual person.

> When the novelist writes of a man "coming to him-self" through some such catalyst as catastrophe or ordeal, he may be offering obscure testimony to a gross disorder of consciousness and to the need of recovering oneself as neither angel nor organism but as a wayfaring creature somewhere between (Percy, *Message*, 113).

In using the word "wayfarer," Percy is speaking of one who is on a journey, alone, searching for his desti-nation, of a God-made being who has a destiny and completion beyond earth, and upon which his individ-uality, sovereignty, and freedom are based. He has gone beyond the existentialism of his European mentors of the old modern age into the cosmological contexts of Teilhard de Chardin and Guardini in his contemplation of the new age.

In order to reach this stage through his novels, it is helpful to trace his characters from the point where Percy himself begins, the alienation of modern man, and through his search, his journey, his discovery, and his hope for the future.

THE MALAISE

The protagonists of all of the novels of Walker Percy suffer from a malaise, a dis-ease of which they have become acutely aware. They are reacting to the feeling of being part of the mass man of modern society explained away by sociologists, behaviorists and psychiatrists. Percy once commented to an interviewer that:

A loss of sovereignty has occurred so that we are more subject to invisible authority—scientists and so forth. We think of what *one* should do in a certain situation, not what *I* should do. Will Barrett in *The Second Coming* is a man who, whatever his faults, has reclaimed sovereignty; he demands to know what it's all about ... (Hobson, "The Study," 53).

His characters evidence their alienation from the idea of mass man in various ways and suffer from both physical and mental manifestations. In *The Moviegoer* Binx Bolling suffers from constant insomnia and shaking terror. Will Barrett of *The Last Gentleman* is given to fits of *déjà vu* and amnesia. The psychiatrist of *Love in the Ruins*, Dr. Thomas More, has "morning terror," disorientation, and suicidal tendencies. Lance Lamar of *Lancelot* loses reality completely and becomes a murderer. The Will Barrett of *The Second Coming* sustains blackouts and entertains suicidal tendencies. All of these symptoms are analyzed away by psychoanalysts and physicians, grist for Percy's deft satire.

Each of these main characters had a father who took his own life, or, as in the case of Binx's father, who died a soldier's death. Only two have mothers who are alive; three are widowers. One—Tom More—has lost a daughter. All are lonely, adrift, or marooned. But however similar their symptoms, they emerge as individual characters, masterfully shaped by nuance and subtlety.

In an epigraph at the beginning of *The Moviegoer* (New York: Alfred A. Knopf, 1961), Percy's first novel and one which won the National Book Award in 1962, he quotes from Kierkegaard's *Sickness unto Death*: "...the specific character of despair is precisely this: it is unaware of being despair." Unconscious despair is at the heart of Binx's malaise. Binx defines this a number of times. "The malaise is the pain of loss. The world is lost to you, the world and the people in it, and there remains only you and the world and you no more able to be in the world than Banquo's ghost" (Percy, *Moviegoer*, 120). What Binx has lost is himself as an individual. He has been careful to receive the certification of his existence and his "wallet is full of identity cards, library cards, credit cards.... It is a pleasure to carry out the duties of a citizen and to receive in return a receipt or a neat styrene card with one's name on it certifying, so to speak, one's right to exist" (Percy, *Moviegoer,* 6-7). Yet these only identify him as part of a group: a citizen, a worker, a consumer. He is only mass man, and therefore lost to himself.

Why should an intelligent, handsome, successful stockbroker, now nearing his thirtieth birthday, despair? He lives deliberately in a modern, pleasant, neutral zone called Gentilly near New Orleans—a zone between his father's old, wealthy Southern family and his mother's new family and middle-class environment. But he really is at home nowhere and his own apartment is situated on Elysian Fields, a road that goes nowhere. He dates his beautiful secretaries, gets briefly caught up in "careless raptures," and goes to the movies.

Binx's "dis-ease" is not due, however, to over-concern with himself. He is acutely aware of everything and everyone about him. He listens to Aunt Emily carefully for a clue as to what he should do, rejecting her stoicism but promising her to make a decision soon about her proposal that he enter medical school and accept accommodations in the carriage house, which she has fixed up for him. He can be counted on to be loyal and attentive to his lovely and tormented cousin Kate. He cultivates friendships with theater owners, ticket clerks, a landlady—aware of their loneliness. In the conduct of his business, he advises his clients about their financial planning in a way that suggests he is personally interested in their well being. All-in-all he is a compassionate man. Yet he is unable to define the void within himself or a future for himself.

Nor is Binx's dislocation due to his participation in

the Korean War in which he was wounded. He bears little resemblance to Hemingway's wounded Frederic Henry of *A Farewell to Arms*, who, horrified by war and death, is incapable of defining the void within himself. Unlike Henry, Binx finds a clue to existence while he is lying wounded in Korea, a clue he later follows.

Binx's dread is "a little vortex of despair, moving through the world like a still eye of a hurricane" (Percy, *Moviegoer*, 121). Using the mechanism of "rotation" (a term Kierkegaard uses), he exchanges his ordinary Dodge used in his outings with his secretaries for an MG. But this does not sustain his well being. He also switches one secretary for another, but still describes his "dis-ease":

> On its way home, the MG becomes infested with malaise. It is not unexpected, since Sunday afternoon is always the worst time for malaise.... A fine Sunday afternoon, though. A beautiful boulevard, ten thousand handsome cars, fifty thousand handsome, well-fed and kindhearted people, and the malaise settles on us like a fall-out (Percy, *Moviegoer*, 166).

So often Walker Percy sounds the common chord, recognizable in all our weeks and days, yet undefined—the Sunday afternoon knell, the unconscious intake of breath, the unnameable dread.

In a marvelously perceptive passage, Percy describes an incident that happens on New Orleans's Royal Street. The Quarter is gearing up for Mardi Gras week, teeming with tourists on the prowl of antique shops and snapping pictures of wrought-iron balconies. Binx becomes particularly alert when he catches sight of William Holden, one of his favorite screen actors, walking down the street. Binx is quick to observe the reaction to Holden of a young, unsophisticated honeymoon couple, threatened and unsure of themselves in this new setting.

> The boy perks up for a second, but seeing Holden doesn't really help him. On the contrary. He can only contrast Holden's resplendent reality with his own shadowy and precarious existence. Obviously he is more miserable than ever (Percy, *Moviegoer,* 16).

But something happens. Holden has stopped to ask some women who "look like housewives from Hattiesburg" for a match, but they have none. Recognizing him, they blush and become confused. Then the young bridegroom springs into action.

> The boy holds out a light, nods briefly to Holden's thanks, then passes on without a flicker of recognition.... The boy has done it! He has won title to his own existence, as plenary an existence now as Holden's, by refusing to be stampeded like the ladies from Hattiesburg. He is a citizen like Holden; two men of the world they are. All at once the world is open to him (Percy, *Moviegoer,* 16).

But Holden turns down "Toulouse, shedding light as he goes," and as soon as he disappears, Binx remarks:

> "Am I mistaken or has a fog of uneasiness, a thin gas of malaise, settled on the street? The businessmen hurry back to their offices, the shoppers to their cars, the tourists to their hotels. Ah, William Holden, we already need you again" (Percy, *Moviegoer,* 18).

What does this mean to Binx? He is not the callow young man but the sophisticated observer, able to grasp the significance of the moment. He experiences something of a breakthrough—he participates in the reestablishment of the young man's sovereignty. Yet, for him, the illumination is momentary; by implication, it is not sustained for the bridegroom either.

Even Binx's strong and positive Aunt Emily acknowledges her own sense of a rift in society, an approaching end to the modern age; what she calls, "the going under of the evening land. . . . I can tell you, my young friend, it is evening. It is very late." Binx realizes that:

> for her too the fabric is dissolving, but for her even the dissolving makes sense. She understands the chaos to come. It seems so plain when I see it through her eyes. My duty in life is simple. I go to medical school. I live a long useful life serving my fellowman. What's wrong with this? All I have to do is remember it (Percy, *Moviegoer*, 54).

Binx's abstraction is such that this does not satisfy him. There must be more. As a seeker he must have *his* reason for doing something. He determines to find it.

*T*he Last Gentleman, the young Will Barrett, is also caught up in the abstract, viewing his life at first introduction as one of "pure possibility." Percy writes, "Like many young men in the South, he became overly subtle and had trouble ruling out the possible" (Walker Percy, *The Last Gentleman* [New York: Farrar, Straus and

Giroux, 1966] 10). His alienation and disorientation were "part of a family pattern":

> Over the years his family had turned ironical and lost its gift for action. It was an honorable and violent family, but gradually the violence had been deflected and turned inward. ... The father was a brave man too and he said he didn't care what others thought, but he did care. More than anything else, he wished to act with honor and to be thought well of by other men. So living for him was a strain. He became ironical. For him it was not a small thing to walk down the street on an ordinary September morning. In the end he was killed by his own irony and sadness and by the strain of living out an ordinary day in a perfect dance of honor.
>
> As for the present young man, the last of the line, he did not know what to think. So he became a watcher and a listener and a wanderer" (Percy, *Last Gentleman*, 9-10).

Will goes to Princeton, occupying the same room as his grandfather and father before him, doing well in his studies and liked by his classmates until one afternoon while the "ghost of his grandfather howled around 203 Lower Pyne" he decides that "this is no place for me for another half hour" (Percy, *Last Gentleman*, 15), and boards a bus for New York. Deciding to live in New York, he returns to the South to settle his family estate, leaving his family home to numerous old aunts.

In New York, he takes a room at the YMCA and finds a job as a humidification engineer at Macy's where he presides over a console of switches during the night in a room three floors below street level. In this, he is like Dostoevsky's underground man and not unlike Binx

Bolling of *The Moviegoer*, who lives in a basement apartment. He is orphaned, alone, unable yet to reach out from his abstraction to reality. Sensing his position and suffering from *déjà vu* and blackouts, he seeks psychoanalysis, which he continues dutifully five days a week for five years. "Even now he made the highest possible scores on the psychological aptitude tests, especially in the area of problem-solving and goal-seeking. The trouble was he couldn't think what to do between tests" (Percy, *Last Gentleman*, 9). He finally decides that the "analyst had got it all wrong. It was not the prospect of the Last Day which depressed him but rather the prospect of living through an ordinary Wednesday morning" (Percy, *Last Gentleman*, 22).

At the end of five years, Will determines to end his therapy. There follows the hilarious episode demonstrating that not only does he have Dr. Gamow baffled, he has picked up so much of the psychiatrist's knowledge that he can turn the tables on him. There is a reversal of position and the doctor becomes paranoid and angry:

> For the thousandth time Dr. Gamow looked at his patient—who sat as usual, alert and pleasant—and felt a small spasm of irritation. It was this amiability, he decided, which got on his nerves. There was a slyness about it and an opacity which put one off. It had not always been so between them. For the first year the analyst had been charmed—never had he had a more responsive patient. Never had his own theories found a readier confirmation than in the free (they seemed to be free) associations and the copious dreams which this one spread out at his feet like so many trophies.... At last the suspicion awoke that he, the doctor, was being *entertained*, royally it is true and getting paid for the

privilege besides, but entertained nevertheless. Trophies they were sure enough, these dazzling wares offered every day, trophies to put him off the scent while the patient got clean away. Sourer still was the second suspicion that even the patient's dreams and recollections, which bore out the doctor's theories, confirmed hypotheses right and left, were somehow or other a performance too, the most exquisite of courtesies, as if the apple had fallen to the ground to please Sir Isaac Newton (Percy, *Last Gentleman*, 30-31).

The psychoanalyst has completely missed Will in his eagerness to place him in a category—he thinks of him as "one" not as "he." He has missed the Southern stoic background, his individuality, and the nature of his problem. And Will, always the gentleman, is always willing to please and to affirm the doctor's theories, is always most adaptable. Yet he hopes for more and continues to come. He himself is "left over." And now, even Dr. Gamow, without realizing the nature of his own inadequacy, can only be irritated with his patient:

The last year of the analysis the doctor had grown positively disgruntled. This one was a Southern belle, he decided, a good dancing partner, light on his feet and giving away nothing. For five years they had danced, the two of them, the strangest dance in history, each attuned to the other and awaiting his pleasure, and so off they went crabwise and nowhere at all (Percy, *Last Gentleman*, 31).

Although Dr. Gamow is exasperated with his patient, the patient has "a high opinion of his analyst," and has only decided to terminate their sessions because he had reached the limits of analysis and sensed a new direction. In a masterful exchange, Percy satirizes modern psychiatric misinterpretations, which are the results of attempts to fit patients into categories. At the end, the analyst is still urging Will to join a new "small group" he is forming. Although Will has told him the truth—that he has run out of funds and must quit, Dr. Gamow decides that his patient is "mad" at him. He himself becomes more and more "mad" as the conversation continues. Forever amiable, Will tries to see his point, but he has made his decision. Percy's subtlety is exquisite:

> At the end of the hour they arose and shook hands pleasantly. The patient took a last look at the dusty hummingbird which had been buzzing away at the same trumpet vine for five years. The little bird seemed dejected. The bird, the print, the room itself had the air of things one leaves behind. It was time to get up and go. He was certain he would never see any of them again (Percy, *Last Gentleman*, 39).

With his newly purchased $1,900 telescope, which will allow him to study things and individuals in depth, he sets out for self-discovery: "Once again he found himself alone in the world, cut adrift from Dr. Gamow, a father of sorts, and from his alma mater, sweet mother psychoanalysis" (Percy, *Last Gentleman*, 39). He is prepared to cope with his temporary amnesia and fits of *déjà vu.*

> I am indeed an engineer, he thought, if only a humidification engineer, which is no great shakes of a profession. But I am also an engineer in a deeper sense: I shall engineer the future of my life according to the scientific principles and self-knowledge I

have so arduously gained from five years of analysis (Percy, *Last Gentleman,* 40).

Will has missed the point himself in crediting science in self-knowledge, yet with his telescope, a scientific instrument designed to extend the viewing power of the human eye, he begins his search for sovereignty.

In *Love in the Ruins*, Tom More is a psychiatrist who anticipates the end of the world. He has invented a device which he hopes, if he can get it accepted, would yet save the world—and win him the Nobel Prize. He is older than Percy's first two protagonists, and torn by the traumas and ironies of life. At the beginning of his successful career as a psychiatrist, he made a breakthrough in a study of heavy sodium radiation and its effect on mental states, and became briefly famous.

When he and his wife lost their only daughter through a painful and disfiguring disease, he fell prey to "morning terror, shook like a leaf at the breakfast table, and began to drink vodka with my grits. At the same time I developed liberal anxiety, I also contracted conservative rage and large-bowel complaints" (Walker Percy, *Love in the Ruins* [New York: Farrar, Straus and Giroux, 1971] 24). Eventually, he loses his wife to a man More describes as a "heathen Englishman," a lecturer on I Ching. Apparently engaged in her own search, she goes with the Englishman to a colony in Mexico, where eventually she dies.

Tom's everydayness is spent in seizures of alternating terror and delight, intermixed with intense longings, which are followed by "extraordinary tranquility of mind, of heightened perception, clairvoyance, and increased inductive powers (Percy, *Love*, 28). During one of these periods, which occurs while he is an inmate in a mental ward, Tom makes the discovery for which he hopes to get the Nobel Prize and save modern humanity from its sickness—the More Qualitative Quantitative Ontological Lapsometer which measures the deep malaise troubling man.

Dr. More is a descendent of St. Thomas More who lost his head for his Catholic faith. Though he styles himself a "bad Catholic" and has lost all but a vestige of belief in his pursuit of science, he frequently recalls his ancestor, "that dearest best noblest merriest of Englishmen," and is proud of his heritage. Wryly he observes:

> By contrast, I am possessed by terror and desire and live a solitary life. My life is a longing, longing for women, for the Nobel Prize, for the hot bosky bite of bourbon whiskey and other great heart-wrenching longings that have no name (Percy, *Love*, 23).

In a series of flashbacks which tell the story, he has also, in his despair, slashed his wrists while watching Perry Como's Christmas show and ended in the same ward which houses some of his patients and where he was inspired with his invention. The novel is set in the near future: "these dread latter days of the old violent beloved U.S.A. and of the Christ-forgetting Christ-haunted death-dealing Western world" (Percy, *Love,* 3). Percy's Tom More is not talking about a future viewed in science-fiction but one that is foreseeable from our "everyday" world. Highways are crumbling, vines resurging through cracks in foundations, motels are abandoned, communities are sectioned, the country is split, religion is sublimated, euthanasia is accepted, and an incipient guerilla war between black and whites exists.

On Sundays in Paradise Estates, where Tom has a beautiful home, the town liberals happily search for the ivory-billed woodpecker while the conservatives attend their watered-down Christian services. In this rare place the liberals (Leftpapasanes) and conservatives (Knotheads) exist side-by-side, whereas in most American towns one or the other seems to be in charge. Near Paradise Estates, in Honey Island Swamp, live the Bantus and an assortment of society's white dropouts. Tom More observes that in the U.S.A. the "center did not hold" (Percy, *Love*, 18). Yet few seem to be aware or to listen to his warnings.

Even though Tom lives comfortably enough he knows "these are bad times," that a catastrophe is about to happen against which he has inoculated himself and three women with whom he expects to survive. A gin-sodden Tom moves the three women into a ruined motel and awaits the cataclysm, faced with his own disorders as well as the perilous state of the world.

L ance Lamar, the anti-hero of *Lancelot*, has disintegrated as a person. In his journey from indifference to violence, he has literally blown away his own past, murdered, and nearly accomplished his own suicide. In making his painful way back to reality as a patient in a mental institution, he tells of the onset of his malaise.

Descendent of a distinguished old Louisiana family, and still lord of Belle Isle, a beautiful plantation home, he was a "man gone to seed." Sometimes lawyer and writer and a former famous football star and Rhodes scholar, he has abandoned his interest in liberal causes, and even in his family: " . . . for the last few years I had done nothing but fiddle at law, fiddle at history, keep up with the news (why?), watch Mary Tyler Moore, and drink myself into unconsciousness every night" (Walker Percy, *Lancelot,* [New York: Farrar, Straus and Giroux, 1977] 60).

Now, looking back on it, he is able to admit his "secret wound"—not being able to make love to his wife, nor discover the reason for it. The clue was a cipher which signified his daughter's blood type on a camp application—the letter "0," indicating that he could not be her father. By implication, it also signifies his own zero state. Instead of shock and anger, the discovery triggers "the worm of interest" in this disintegrated man. Lance immediately drops his seedy appearance and his drinking habits and becomes alive again, bent on his quest for the "sin." He had loved his wife, Margot, a Texan, and had allowed her to restore his home and make him over in the image of an old Southern plantation owner. After this was accomplished, she had lost interest In Lance and had become involved in acting and making a movie at Belle Isle.

Lance's past unfolds in his conversations with an old friend, now a priest-psychiatrist, who visits him. The growth of his malaise from his spectacular beginnings in college to his present decadence becomes apparent. He lacks something to live for. Having sliced the old Southern ethic of the past from his life, he has nothing to fill the void. Now, with his knowledge of betrayal, he is a purely negative thrust. The beauties and glory of the past become tarnished and corroded like his bowie knife. The negative aspect, the perverse part of his mentality, is detailed in this passage:

A new life. I began a new life over a year ago when I walked out of that dark parlor after leaving the supper table. Or rather walked into that dark parlor.

. . . . As I stepped into the parlor with its smell of lemon wax and damp horsehair, I stopped and shut my eyes a moment to get used to the darkness. Then as I crossed the room to the sliding doors, something moved in the corner of my eye. It was a man at the far end of the room. He was watching me. He did not look familiar. There was something wary and poised about the way he stood, shoulders angled, knees slightly bent as if he were prepared for anything. He was mostly silhouette but white on black like a reversed negative. His arms were long, one hanging lower and lemur-like from dropped shoulder. His head was cocked, turned enough so I could see the curve at the back. There was a sense about him of a vulnerability guarded against, an overcome gawkiness, a conquered frailty. Seeing such a man one thought first: Big-headed smartboy type; then thought again: But he's big too. If he hadn't developed his body, worked out, he'd have a frail neck, two tendons, and a hollow between, balancing that big head. He looked like a long-distance runner who had conquered polio. He looked like a smart sissy rich boy who has devoted his life to getting over it.

Then I realized it was myself reflected in the dim pier mirror (Percy, *Lancelot,* 63-64).

The reversed image, the "negative" photograph, and the fact that Lancelot is a stranger to himself, complete his disintegration as a person. He next appears as a knight inhabited by a demon as in Arthurian tales.

The gentle, bemused Will Barrett of *The Second Coming* is bent only on his own destruction. His is an inner weakness. He has lost the conviction of the meaning of life, and his earlier malaise, now augumented by experience, has blossomed anew. The rich, unattractive wife he married to make her happy has died, and his self-reliant daughter is about to be married. Still in his forties, he has retired from his successful Wall Street law practice and returned to North Carolina and the golf course. Always an exceptional golfer, his distraction now causes him to develop a nasty slice and he blacks out unexpectedly in bunkers. As he searches in the bordering woods for his balls, he is confronted by *déjà vu*, another malady of the past, and a particular incident in the past which he has never been able to resolve—his father's suicide. In the woods he also encounters the peculiar woodland person who has recently escaped from a psychiatric hospital where she was "buzzed" into amnesia.

In the footsteps of his father, Will contemplates suicide: "First it was only a thought that popped into his head. Next, it was an idea he entertained ironically. Finally, it was a course of action which he took seriously and decided to carry out." Why? He comes up with generalizations:

> It astonished him that as farcical as most people's lives were, they generally gave no sign of it. Why was it that it was he not they who had decided to shoot himself? How did they manage to deceive themselves and even appear to live normally, work as usual, play golf, tell jokes, argue politics? Was he crazy or was it rather the case that other people went to any length to disguise from themselves the

fact that their lives were farcical? He couldn't decide (Walker Percy, *The Second Coming* [New York: Farrar, Straus and Giroux, 1980] 4).

Echoes of this modern existential man contemplating the absurdity of life are, of course, found in other novels. Dostoevsky's Ivan Karamazov is tortured by loneliness in his search for meaning. Sartre's Roquentin is a recluse who is reduced to cynical observation of his fellow man. Updike's Rabbit runs to find life but only finds emptiness.

What distinguishes Percy's protagonists from these characters is that they are still alive enough to catch a fleeting flash of hope, a hint of another possibility, a question unanswered, a further interest, care for another individual. Binx Bolling responds to Kate's predicament; young Will Barrett to Jamie's illness; Tom More to his concern for all mankind; Lance Lamar is enlivened by a negative reaction becoming unexpectedly positive; and the older Will Barrett, by a question unanswered and a chance encounter with someone who needs help. In each case something serves to spark the character's search for meaning.

THE SEARCH

he idea of a search first occurs to Binx Bolling (*The Moviegoer*) when he regains consciousness after being shot in Korea and notices a dung beetle "scratching around under the leaves." It is the experience of seeing things anew. It happens again as he examines his pile of pocket items on his bureau and sees them for the first time. "They might have belonged to someone else" (Percy, *Moviegoer*, 11). It is this flip of recognition which sets him on the search. Because he is anyone, he is not himself. He further defines it this way:

> The search is what anyone would undertake if he were not sunk in the everydayness of his own life. This morning, for example, I felt as if I had come to

myself on a strange island. And what does such a
castaway do? Why, he pokes around the neighbor-
hood and he doesn't miss a trick.

His mind leaps onward. "To become aware of the possibility of the search is to be onto something. Not to be
onto something is to be in despair" (Percy, *Moviegoer*,
13). Now, he has not only seen the neutral zone in which
he has been operating but has witnessed what can come
of it: despair. Percy quotes Kierkegaard in the prologue
to *The Moviegoer*: " . . . the specific character of despair
is precisely this: it is unaware of being despair." This
unconscious despair is at the heart of the malaise and
its realization; it is likewise the springboard to the per-
ceptions which lead to the search.

When Binx poses the question: "What do you
seek—God? you ask with a smile," Binx's attitude is
serious, not facetious (Percy, *Moviegoer*, 13). He continues to explore, citing the opinion polls of mass man,
according to which 98% of the population are believers.
"Have 98% of Americans already found what I seek or
are they so sunk in everydayness that not even the
possibility of a search has occurred to them?" (Percy,
Moviegoer, 14). Without verbalizing it, what Percy's
character seems to be saying is that perhaps the 98%
have accepted, not discovered, God, and have abandoned the day-to-day search for that God and the meaning of existence that is matter for intense investigation—the purpose of a lifetime, not secured once and
then forgotten. It can be lost, such as in Binx's case, or
rediscovered and intensified—an active pursuit of
many dimensions—as in the case of Will Barrett and
of Lancelot.

Binx is a moviegoer because the movies are "onto
the search," and so constitute a part of his wandering,

part of his investigation, even if, according to Binx, "they screw it up." Movies may set their hero or heroine on a search, but at the end they leave them sunk in the same "everydayness," no longer searching. Even so, Binx himself makes use of them for what they do, how they inspire and provide new perspectives. He is fond of seeing a movie again and again, of remembering and finding clues of his past experiences in viewing them. The movies become part of his search, just as everyone he sees or meets become part of it. He has an intense awareness of life, which he shares with Kate, whom he hopes to snatch from the pit of her despair.

His search is at first "vertical"—viewing life from the perspective of universe—a scientific investigation emanating from his reading. He realizes he may have discovered the universe, but "I myself was left over." He progresses to what he calls his "horizontal" search, which causes him to "wander seriously and sit and read as a diversion." He constantly looks for clues not only in movies but in his past—from the Southern aristocratic paternal side of his family, from his mother's hard-working-class family, and from his half-brothers and sisters. What makes Binx unlike so many other existentialist heroes or anti-heroes, is that his search is not merely a self-centered investigation. He has great compassion for each person he touches. He seems to understand even those with whom he does not agree, and his ironic observations are warmed with compassion.

And there I have lived ever since, solitary and in wonder, wondering day and night, never a moment without wonder. Now and then my friends stop by, all gotten up as young eccentrics with their beards and bicycles, and down they go into the Quarter to hear some music and find some whores and still I wish them well. As for me, I stay home with Mrs. Schexnaydre and turn on TV. Not that I like TV so much, but it doesn't distract me from the wonder. That is why I can't go to the trouble they go to. It is distracting, and not for five minutes will I be distracted from the wonder (Percy, *Moviegoer*, 42).

In the second novel, *The Last Gentleman*, Will Barrett's search is for himself, for an identity culled from his field of limitless possibility. Wiped out personally, financially, and psychologically, Will begins his search with a $1,900 telescope he has purchased by withdrawing the last of his savings. To Will, the Tetzler has "magical properties" and penetrates "to the heart of things" (Percy, *Last Gentleman*, 28).

He sets up his telescope in Central Park where he had earlier become fascinated by a peregrine. The symbol of the hawk becomes more clear as the novel proceeds. Percy develops it most subtly as a symbol of the spiritual. Here, like a coin is flipped from eagle to human head, the writer flips with natural grace from search for the hawk to beautiful girl.

In his search for Kitty, who, he finds, is even more at odds with herself than he, he encounters her family. Her younger brother Jamie, terminally ill, then becomes his focus. As Will telescopes outside himself, he is drawn into the problems of others, allowing these currents to carry him into fresh discoveries for himself along the way. Sensing that Jamie's time for a search is very short, Will presents his telescope to the youth as a birthday present. When the Vaught family decides to travel South after Jamie's series of treatments is over, and his father invites Will to go with them as a companion to Jamie, he agrees to do so. There are a number of mishaps but eventually he is reunited with the Vaughts and continues to be the engineer in their destinies as well as in his own. This fascination subconsciously takes precedence over his love for Kitty.

When Will meets the elder Vaught son, Sutter, a physician, he discovers that Sutter is on a search of sorts, except that his search is directed not to life but to death. During the previous year Sutter had involved Jamie in a search that nearly ended in death for both of them somewhere in the Mexican desert. Yet Will is intrigued by Sutter's intellect and experience. Sutter, the existentialist who has found only dead ends and despair, is unable to help his younger brother find meaning; he is content that Will try.

Will also encounters Jamie's unattractive sister, Val, who has given up her doctoral studies to join the Catholic Faith. She has entered a religious order and will teach a community of Tyree black outcasts in Alabama. Will resents her abrasive, positive attitude and rejects out-of-hand her charge of responsibility for Jamie's baptism. He is only interested in easing Jamie's life, not providing for his death. Yet, after an accidental blow on the head causes him to experience total amnesia and separates him from Jamie and Kitty, it is Val who helps him reestablish his identity and provides direction for his ultimate search. For as long as his interest in others deepens, the end of one search must always give rise to another.

Early in the novel, Percy introduces several incidents which illustrate that Will's growth progresses as a result of catastrophes and his ensuing concern with the plight of others. One such incident involves his finding a lost child during a hurricane and his returning her to her family before her disappearance is discovered. Another such significant catastrophe takes place on Will's visit to a New York art museum. Assaulted by his own loss of identity, Will is not able to experience the paintings, not even through the enjoyment of other viewers, when suddenly a workman repairing a skylight overhead comes crashing down and is buried in debris. Will and a family nearby are covered with dust. No one is hurt but the workman, who has been knocked out.

> Suddenly everyone remembered the worker. They knelt beside him and bore him up like the mourners of Count Orgaz. The workman, an Italian youth with sloe-black eyes and black mustache who was as slight as Charlie Chaplin in his coveralls, opened his eyes and began stretching up his eyebrows as if he were trying to stay awake. Others came running up. The workman was not bleeding but he could not get his breath. As they held him and he gazed up at them, it was as if he were telling them that he could not remember how to breathe. Then he pulled himself up on the engineer's arm and air came sucking into his throat just grudgingly permitting it.
>
> It was at this moment that the engineer happened to look under his arm and catch sight of the Velasquez. It was glowing like a jewel! The painter might have just stepped out of his studio and the engineer, passing in the street, had stopped to look through the open door. The painting could be seen (Percy, *Last Gentleman*, 27).

Will's involvement with the worker's mortal crisis and the subsequent joy at his victory allows him to transcend his everydayness and grasp the moment for himself. The simplicity and elegance of Percy's style are brilliantly conjoined to illustrate and substantiate Will's ongoing search.

Tom More in *Love in the Ruins* thinks he has found meaning in his scientific search for man's integrity in a modern world about to self-destruct. More seeks a scientific breakthrough to deflect the disaster. He has not yet discovered that science cannot heal the whole man, just as he cannot heal himself of lust, alcoholism, and despair. His hope has become desperation. But, as ever in Percy, the coin of science and matter has a flip side which carries the head image of the whole Thomas; eventually it lands this side up. It is the Caesar coin of the Bible. When Tom surrenders the use of his invention to the devil, personified by Art Immelmann, in exchange for the Nobel Prize, he can see the danger. Only then does he move to avert disaster.

After his daughter died and his wife left him, Thomas gave up any spiritual search. He had found God in the Catholic Church, but when he lost Samantha and their shared joy in belief, he sank into despair and lost all interest in religion. His wife, Doris, set off to find a belief on her own, telling him: "You're not a seeker after the truth. You think you have the truth, and what good does it do you?" (Percy, *Love*, 70). Tom speaks ruefully of his previously happy religious experience:

> . . . I went to mass with Samantha, happy as a man could be, ate Christ and held him to his word, if you

eat me you'll have life in you, so I had life in me. After mass we'd walk home to Paradise through the violet evening ... and I'd skip with happiness, cut the fool like David while Samantha told elephant jokes, go home, light the briquets ... singing "Tantum Ergo" and "Deh vieni alla finestra" from *Don Giovanni* and, while Samantha watched Gentle Ben, invite Doris out under the Mobile pinks, Doris as lusty and merry a wife then as a man could have, a fine ex-Episcopal ex-Apple Queen from the Shenandoah Valley (Percy, *Love*, 138).

Then his daughter contracts a horribly disfiguring disease and dies. He still believes, but he stops his search for God and concentrates on a search for a cure for the psychic ills of mankind, the discovery of which should return him to an Edenic state:

Suppose I could hit on the right dosage and weld that broken self whole! What if man could reenter paradise, so to speak, and live there both as man and spirit, whole and intact man-spirit, as solid flesh as a speckled trout, a dappled thing, yet aware of itself as a self! (Percy, *Love*, 36).

So the modern Thomas dreams and searches for a Utopia not as aware of its impossibility as the ancestor he symbolizes.

Since Percy has called his next novel *Lancelot*, the obvious parallels to the Arthurian legend must be considered. But Percy is never merely obvious. His Lancelot is not the proud, pure knight of the legend; he is like a photographic negative of the hero—a seedy, sodden, vanquished knight of despair. He is both the lover Lancelot and the cuckolded,saddened King Arthur. His quest is not for the Holy Grail, but a perverse one—a search for the "unholy Grail." His Percival is a priest-psychiatrist, an old college friend, who is present primarily to hear his "confession." And Merlin is his betrayer, not his mentor. His "Ex Caliber" is his bowie knife, which may not be authentic.

Lancelot Andrewes Lamar's search, a form of despair, is a completely negative one. Born of the cipher "0," it is a nothing and, like anti-matter, spawns a terrible violence. This search details another of Percy's paradoxes: Lamar is searching for evil in the negative hope of finding good, God. The "0" is the blood type of his daughter's birth certificate and the proof that he is not her father. This fact piques in him not anger, but a "turning of the worm of interest" just strong enough to save him from his previous disintegration and despair.

> In the space of one evening I had made the two most important discoveries of my life. I discovered my wife's infidelity and five hours later I discovered my own life. I saw it and myself clearly for the first time.
>
> Can good come from evil? Have you ever considered the possibility that one might undertake a search not for God but for evil? . . .
>
> In times when nobody is interested in God, what would happen if you could prove the existence of sin, pure and simple? Wouldn't that be a windfall for you? A new proof of God's existence! If there is such a thing as sin, evil, a living malignant force, there must be a God (Percy, *Lancelot*, 51-52).

Thus we have Lance's concept of a search for the Holy Grail. He is the anti-hero par excellence. The impure knight of tarnished armor and negative purpose. His quest both saves him from complete despair and hastens his psychotic rampage. The sin, of course, is his wife's repeated infidelity and all of his energy and purpose and ingenuity go into planning the revelation and consequences.

> ... there is no pain on this earth like seeing the same woman look at another man the way she once looked at you.
>
> Do you know what jealousy is? Jealousy is an alteration in the very shape of time itself. Time loses its structure. Time stretches out. She isn't here. Where is she? Who is she with? (Percy, *Lancelot*, 122-23).

In another passage Lancelot confesses, "The thought of Margot dead was painful but not intolerable. But Margot under another man ..." (Percy, *Lancelot*, 16). The beast he discovers and confronts is of such proportions that he reacts with cold rage born of madness. His own survival is accidental. Out of his survival he has a stirring of hope. And his search continues.

In *The Second Coming*, the older Will Barrett has run out of reasons to live. His wife has died, his daughter is about to get married, and he has retired from his law career. His old illness is getting worse. He begins his search by researching his father's suicide. His fascination with it nearly breeds imitation. Yet he deems his father's suicide a waste.

... It availed nothing, proved nothing, solved nothing, posed no questions let alone answered questions, did nobody good. It was no more than an exit, a getting up and going out, a closing of a door.

Most of all, it offended Will Barrett's sense of economy and proportion, of thrift, that so much, a life no less, could be spent with so little return ...

I will not waste mine, he thought, smiling (Percy, *Second Coming*, 182).

Rather than a search for oblivion, he seeks the answer to Pascal's wager on the existence of God. He wishes to "settle the question of God once and for all (Percy, *Second Coming,* 186).

With his retirement from a Wall Street law firm, he has returned to his home in "the most Christian nation in the world, the U.S.A., in the most Christian part of that nation, the South, in the most Christian state in the South, North Carolina, in the most Christian town in North Carolina" (Percy, *Second Coming*, 13). Yet the question that remains on his mind is the existence of God. To him the absence of Jews in North Carolina becomes more a sign of God's departure than the many kinds of Christian churches are a sign of His presence.

His millions, his Rolls and Mercedes, his expertise at golf, no longer provide him comfort or peak his interest. Haunted by the ghost of his father's suicide, Will Barrett becomes no patient pilgrim, willing to endure and wait, but a challenger to God, if he exists, for an immediate response. In his search he has divided people into two categories: believers and unbelievers: "The first are the believers, who think they know the reason why we find ourselves in this ludicrous predicament yet act for all the world as if they don't. The second are the unbelievers, who don't know the reason and don't care if they don't" (Percy, *Second Coming*, 190). He considers himself an unbeliever but he demands an explanation; he must be certain that there is no God. He devises an elaborate plan which is to be the exemplum of Pascal's wager and climbs into a grave of his own making. The outcome of this preposterous plan is pure Percyan comedy at its best; Will is forcefully ejected back into life and reintroduced to its sweetness. From an Edenic forest which suggests the painting of Hieronymus Bosch, he is forced to begin the search afresh, this time informed with love, with a partner also searching.

THE JOURNEY

n Percy's novels there is the feeling of a journey, of a progress, of his characters being in search of something. His protagonists are wayfarers, pilgrims, who start from a specific point, who sometimes are temporarily lost or snagged on shallows, but who are always struggling to move toward something. In that sense, the movement is more positive than that of the existential uninformed floating journey described by other modern writers such as Hemingway and Updike. Nor is it the classic water-journey in which the hero finds maturity, such as occurs in *Huckleberry Finn* or *Moby-Dick*. Theirs is not the pure, unlimiting freedom of a water journey that leads to discovery of new places and new persons, and involves events unencumbered by the

past. Percy's characters often travel in reverse, into the past, to discover new clues of their lives, clues that will help to recover the future.

In *The Moviegoer*, Binx Bolling trudges through the impedimental everydayness of consciousness, combining past and present to make something of the future. He must face painful challenges: a charge by his traditional aunt to "make a contribution" as a Southern gentleman; the cry for help by his disturbed cousin Kate; the probing questions of his crippled half-brother Lonnie. Living his vacuous life as a stockbroker in the neutral zone of Gentilly, he escapes these challenges temporarily, but goes nowhere. Only through their resolution is he able to move toward a future.

In the midst of Mardi Gras in New Orleans, he departs with Kate for Chicago on a journey by train, the significance of which rivals that of Thomas Wolfe's hero in *Look Homeward, Angel*. It is a journey through the darkest nights of the spirit to find a first glimmer of hope. Among the ashes of Ash Wednesday, the coals of love glow.

The journey of "two malaisians," as Binx calls it, conceived in a desperate moment of Kate's need to escape, is a journey through darkness. It is a flight of the disembodied rather than that of free spirits. Ten years have passed since Binx has last enjoyed "the peculiar gnosis of trains, stood on the eminence from which there is revealed both the sorry litter of the past and the future bright and simple as can be, and the going itself, one's privileged progress through the world" (Percy, *Moviegoer*, 184). But it was not to be so. Both he and Kate have brought their malaise with them as unwanted baggage. Binx observes the Metier graveyard as they pass and perceives it as a city full of the dead; Kate finds pleasure in the sight of the deserted Capitol building, the moon illuminating its emptiness. She has her nembutol and Binx his flask. Yet together they find some solace in commitment. Their lovemaking, so desperately needed by Kate, is accomplished without passion, but with tremendous compassion and love. Binx remarks:

> The burden was too great and flesh poor flesh, neither hallowed by sacrament nor despised by spirit (for despising is not the worst fate to overtake the flesh), but until this moment seen through and canceled, rendered null by the cold and fishy eye of the malaise—flesh poor flesh now at this moment summoned all at once to be all and everything, end all and be all, the last and only hope quails and fails (Percy, *Moviegoer*, 200).

In another of Percy's paradoxes, Binx is given to a faint joy as he confesses: "The highest moment of a malaisian's life can be that moment when he manages to sin like a proper human (Look at us, Binx—my vagabond friends as good as cried out to me—we're sinning! We're succeeding! We're human after all!)" (Percy, *Moviegoer*, 200-201). There is both the implication of modern society's disavowal of the sins of the flesh and the idea that only a being with body and soul can sin; the union of both proves humanity.

With Kate at peace, Binx confronts "the genie-soul of Chicago," which "flaps down like a buzzard and perches on my shoulder" (Percy, *Moviegoer*, 201). Binx has been to Chicago before:

> ... the wind and the space, they are the genie-soul. The wind flows in steady from the Lake and claims the space for its own, scouring every inch of the

pavements and the cold stony fronts of the buildings. It presses down between buildings, shoulder-
ing them apart in skyey fields of light and air. The
air is wind-pressed into a lens, magnifying and
sharpening and silencing—everything is silenced
in the uproar of the wind that comes ransacking
down out of the North. This is a city where no one
dares dispute the claim of the wind and the skyey
space to the out-of-doors. This Midwestern sky is
the nakedest loneliest sky in America. To escape it,
people live inside and underground (Percy, *Moviegoer*, 203).

Binx had met that "genie-soul" with his father on
another trip. This visit recalls his father's attempt and
need to get close to his son, and the boy's rejection of
him:

> . . . we came, my father and I, to the Field Museum,
> a long dismal peristyle dwindling away into the
> howling distance, and inside stood before a tableau
> of Stone Age Man—father, mother, and child
> crouched around an artificial ember in postures of
> minatory quiet—until, feeling my father's eyes on
> me, I turned and saw what he required of me—very
> special father and son we were that summer, he
> staking his everything this time on a perfect com-
> radship—and I, seeing in his eyes the terrible re-
> quest, requiring from me his very life; I, through a
> child's cool perversity or some atavistic recoil
> from an intimacy too intimate, turned him down,
> turned away, refused him what I knew I could not
> give (Percy, *Moviegoer*, 204).

Here Binx reveals his conviction that he was partly
to blame for his father's loss of desire to live, of his own

failure to love enough. This realization reinforces his renewed commitment to all who love him, especially Kate. When the journey ends with a curt summons from home, the two pilgrims return to face a homecoming mixed with the humility of Ash Wednesday.

The thrust of *The Last Gentleman*, Percy's "rite of passage" novel, is the journey of life, tragic and comic both in the normal course of things. Begun as a pursuit of Kitty, returning with her family to their home in the South, Will's journey is at first jolted into the comic tangent caused by his temporary amnesia, which comes and goes throughout the story. After missing the Vaughts, with whom he was to travel south, Will's wanderings depict a fluidity somewhat akin to Huckleberry Finn's. The bus he leaves New York with was "a stained old Greyhound with high portholes. The passengers sat deep in her hold.... Under the Hudson River she roared, swaying like a schooner" (Percy, *Last Gentleman*, 118). When he departs the bus, Will gets a ride with Forney Aiken, who drives his Chevrolet so that it begins "rowboating badly." Aiken is a white photographer disguised as a Negro in order to provoke a story on discrimination in the South. This, too, might be an ironic parallel to Huck's black companion, Jim. At a stop in Levittown, Will is taken for a realtor by homeowners, and Aiken, for his black client. There is a scuffle before Aiken reveals himself to be white. When all parties to the incident, except Will, take the incident merely as a case of mistaken identity, Percy's satire becomes apparent. Aiken and his writer friend seem to indicate that only Southern prejudice is their aim. Will, the Southerner, is sensitive to it no matter where it occurs.

Will continues his trip south with a carful of female golfers on holiday, arriving in Williamsburg just in time to catch up with the Vaughts. This high-spirited, if brief, episode of the journey introduces what, for Percy, is a recurring locus of Southern life—the golf course. In several of the novels, especially this one and *The Second Coming*, it is the landscape of much of the action. The only novel in which a golf course is not prominent is the first, *The Moviegoer*, which has in its stead another popular Southern setting, Mardi Gras.

Percy's affluent characters live in homes on the fringes of golf courses. The green is the terrain of the good life, carefully tended, groomed, protected. The club is a closed, sweet society, where the most lordly of recreations becomes a serious ritualistic dance and where blacks are properly servants and caddies. Percy describes this magic in *The Last Gentleman*:

The sixth hole fairway of the second nine ran in front of the castle. It had got to be the custom after teeing off to mark the balls and veer over to the patio, where David, the butler, had toddies ready. Custom also required that the talk, unlike other occasions, be serious, usually about politics but sometimes even about philosophical questions. The tone of the sixth-hole break was both pessimistic and pleasureable. The world outlook was bad, yes, but not so bad that it was not a pleasant thing to say so of a gold-green afternoon, with a fair sweat up and sugared bourbon that tasted as good as it smelled. Over yonder, a respectful twenty yards away, stood the caddies, four black ragamuffins who had walked over the ridge from the city and now swung the drivers they took from the great

compartmented, zippered, pocketed, studded, bon-
neted golf bags.

The golfers gazed philosophically into their
whiskey and now and then came out with solemn
Schadenfreude things, just like four prosperous
gents might have done in old Virginny in 1774
(Percy, *Last Gentleman,* 184-85).

This golden tone alters only in the futuristic novel,
Love in the Ruins, where everything is awry. The golf
course bunkers catch fire. The greens become the landscape where Tom is sniped at and where he meets the
world in the form of the revolution, the flesh in the form
of Lola, and the devil in the form of Art Immemann who
offers him his life's ambition, the Nobel Prize.

In *The Last Gentleman*, the golf course still repre-
sents the best of all possible worlds. Will's expertise as
a golfer is the basis of his complete acceptance by Mr.
Vaught. Yet young Jamie who is at the outer edge of life,
finds it intolerable, and is anxious to move on. He is at
least subconsciously aware of his condition, and Will is
willing to move on along the old Tidewater in the camp-
er, "sleeping in the piney woods or along the salt
marshes, rendezvousing with the Cadillac in places like
Wilmington and Charleston" (Percy, *Last Gentleman,*
153).

To Will, this is already home, a part of the South,
even though he has never been at that particular place
before. He has easy conversation with a gas station
owner "in the complex Southern tactic of assaying a
sort of running start, a joke before the joke, ten assump-
tions shared and a common stance of rhetoric and a
whole shared set of special ironies and opposites. He
was home" (Percy, *Last Gentleman*, 154). He was home,
but still journeying and far to go.

"The South he came home to was different from the South he had left. It was happy, victorious, Christian, rich, patriotic and Republican" (Percy, *Last Gentleman,* 177). This "formidable" happiness disconcerts him. "The South was at home. Therefore his homelessness was much worse in the South because he had expected to find himself at home there" (Percy, *Last Gentleman,* 178).

When Jamie expresses a desire to study mathematics, Will enrolls both of them at the university. Kitty decides to join them and happily buries herself in the campus social life. The engineer loses all synchronization with Kitty's and his own feelings, focusing only on Jamie's urgent needs:

> The difference between me and him, thought the engineer and noticed for the first time a slight translucence at the youth's temple, is this: like me he lives in the sphere of the possible, all antenna, ear cocked and lips parted. But I am conscious of it, know what is up, and he is not and does not. He is pure aching primary awareness and does not even know that he doesn't know it (Percy, *Last Gentleman*, 155).

Keeping his promise to Jamie eventually fulfills his own purpose, but not until the tandem ride with the Vaughts is split and each wheel goes off on a tangent trip of its own. Will's journey becomes his own after a blow on the head worsens his amnesia and he follows every clue to his own identity, a road that eventually leads him to his own birthplace and home. There he is confronted again with the spectre of his father's suicide. In that attic, instead of the shotgun, last used by his father on himself, Will chooses a rubber boat in

which he escapes down the Mississippi, accepting the
whole of life as a continuing odyssey, his ultra-sensory
antennae wung-out like sails to catch any inspiration,
any hint of purpose, end or meaning. He has rejected his
father's choice. Even after he has satisfied and complet-
ed his responsibility to Jamie, he resumes the journey
in a progressive mode. This is not just a "rite of passage" from youth to adulthood, but a serious search for
the whole of life.

Tom More of *Love in the Ruins*, in a moment of discovery during an emotional agony, cries "... it is
pilgrims we are, wayfarers on a journey, not pigs, nor
angels" (Percy, *Love,* 109). Even though he pursues an
absolute scientific cure for modern man's psychic illness, Doctor More returns again and again to this belief
of life as a journey, a spiritual progress, negating his
sense of a one-time cure. But since he can diagnose a
man's malaise with his lapsometer and since he considers the end of the world near at hand, he desperately
seeks an instant remedy.

The fiction's action covers a journey of four days
over familiar and limited terrain. Tom is tracked by a
sniper. He is flushed from his enclosed patio and breakfast of duck eggs and vodka, and escapes with revolver
and on foot, since his car no longer works. Repairmen
are nonexistent in the future world he inhabits, so cars,
refrigerators and other equipment are abandoned. His
course in avoiding the sniper crisscrosses from his tryst
in an abandoned motel where he deposits the three
women he loves, to office, hospital, clinic, golf course
and back again. In the apocalypse he envisions, he is

working alone without rest, but not without alcohol, to save the various split community groups, all of which he has entrance to but which do not communicate with each other, from the cataclysm he alone foresees. The sniper fastens onto him like a fly on fly-paper as they journey over the golf course, parts of which are overrun with vines—Paradise is indeed beginning to crumble and nature, rampant, to resurge. In addition, Art Immelmann appears, offering federal funds for the perfection of his invention and assuring him the Nobel Prize if he signs away the rights to the lapsometer's use.

As he treks on, his accomplishments are private: he saves a love child in the swamp from dehydration; he aids a marriage, he soothes an old friend's mental turmoil with his lapsometer, but he cannot convince his colleagues or the hospital director to endorse his lapsometer. In a moment of despair and alcoholic confusion, he signs away his soul—by now it is obvious who Immelmann is—for the Nobel.

Finally, on the third day, in the annual demonstration for staff and medical students, he confronts the spectre of Euthanasia, an accepted practice of his time. His enemy is Dr. Bud Brown, a congenial "quality-of-lifer," who contends that Tom's patient and friend, Mr. Ives, is ready for the Happy Isles Separation Center and the Euphoric switch with which his existence will be terminated. Dr. More and his lapsometer release Mr. Ives from his state of paralysis so that he is able to pursue his inventive career. Tom is the victor, but in his moment of triumph, Immelmann has passed out all of the lapsometers to students and staff. The consequences are chaotic and the crowd disperses. Percy, at his satiric best in this hilarious sequence, mows down behaviorists and "quality-of-lifers"; in fact, he levels the whole of modern scientism.

The last leg of his journey is to stop a revolution between black and white and opposing political factions, a memorable ordeal. The Bantus have captured the Paradise Country Club and after he secures his mother, who lives on its edge, Tom scouts the territory through ditch and then by floating down the river in a stolen pirogue to the clubhouse, where he is finally caught by his Bantu sniper. After an internment in the abandoned Catholic Church in temperatures reminiscent of Purgatory, he manages an escape with a twist of St. Michael's sword, bursting out an air duct "feet first, born again, ejected into the hot bright perilous world . . ." (Percy, *Love*, 311).

In spite of the success of his invention, Tom cannot save anyone, even himself, and he has not grasped the reason why this is so. His efforts dissolve before him, as he contemplates the whole scene from his lookout until the gin fizzes he has been imbibing cause him to black out. The act which saves him is his prayer for help when the soul of his true love is threatened. His humility and acknowledgement of free will give him back his own sovereignty. Art Immelmann disappears into the smoke of the burning bunker.

The real journey for Lancelot, after his vengeful passage as part of the hurricane, causing death and destruction but not accomplishing his own, is the trek backwards in time to recover his own reality and a reason for survival. With his old friend, now psychiatrist-priest Percival, he begins his pilgrimage. Lance confides to Percival:

> Some years ago I discovered that I had nothing to say to anybody nor anybody to me, that is, anything

> worth listening to. There is nothing left to say. So I
> stopped talking. Until you showed up. I don't know
> why I want to talk to you or what I need to tell you
> or need to hear from you. There is something . . .
> (Percy, *Lancelot*, 85).

With his renewal of communication, circumspect at
first, but becoming more and more open, Lance crawls
back out of the cave of psychosis where he had met his
dragon and had been wounded by his own sword of
hate. Along the way he encounters the beautiful subter-
ranean pools of his love of his wife, Margot, and their
mutual pleasure in each other. Little sunlit passages of
memory contain his joy in his first wife, Lucy. He also
discovers fetid pockets of slime—secret sins of his par-
ents he had come upon in childhood. He trips upon the
skeletons—death of his first wife, betrayal by his second, the seduction of his daughter which had shocked
him into unreality. Only with his old friend is he able to
see his way out again and to acknowledge what he has
done. During these passages in memory he even admits
that his kind of retribution is done by "crazies." But
even at this point he is still saying to his friend, "You are
pale as a ghost. What did you whisper? Love? That I am
full of hatred, anger? Don't talk to me of love until we
shovel out the shit" (Percy, *Lancelot*, 179). He is not yet
ready to listen, but is aware first derisively, then with
more consideration, of Percival and the faith he repre-
sents:

> There are only three ways to go. One is their way
> out there, the great whorehouse and fagdom of
> America. I won't have it. The second way is sweet
> Baptist Jesus and I won't have that. Christ, if heav-
> en is full of Southern Baptists, I'd rather rot in hell

with Saladin and Achilles. There is only one way
and we could have had it if you Catholics hadn't
blown it: the old Catholic way. I Lancelot and you
Percival, the only two to see the Grail if you recall.
Did you find the Grail? You don't look like it. Then
we knew what a woman should be like, your Lady,
and what a man should be like, your Lord. I'd have
fought for your Lady because Christ had the
broadsword. Now you've gotten rid of your lady
and taken the sword from Christ.

I won't have it. I won't have it your way or
their way. I won't have it your way with your God-
bless-everything-because-it's-good-only-don't-
but-if-you-do-it's-not-so-bad (Percy, *Lancelot*, 176-
77).

In this trek out of darkness, Percy gives us no response
by Percival to Lancelot's tirades of hate. Lance does not
yet realize that the roars of the evil beast he seeks are
his own. Percival by listening and listening draws Lance
further and further from the despair, hate, and anger
which almost demolishes him until Lance begins to
hear himself. As Lance becomes more and more preoc-
cupied with what is going on beyond himself, he and
Percival begin to burst through the tunnel into the light
of community which lies beyond.

A journey into the cave is the method of resolution
that the aging Will Barrett elects in *The Second
Coming*. His cave is a physical one and his journey
premeditated: to resolve the issue of God's existence.
Will Barrett is willing to stake his own future existence

on it. He feels life is not worth living without the possibility of God and devises an ingenious plan which will either prove God's presence or, if his absence, will make his death appear to be an accident, not a suicide. He accomplishes neither.

He plans his sortie carefully, having settled his responsibility to his daughter. His responsibility to himself remains. Will, in his state of comic madness, determines that God must reveal Himself to Will in a cave he has explored in childhood. He takes no food or water with him, but he does supply himself with his prescribed sleeping pills.

> Madness! Madness! Madness! Yet such was the nature of Will Barrett's peculiar delusion when he left his comfortable home atop a pleasant Carolina mountain and set forth on the strangest adventure of his life, descended into Lost Cove cave looking for proof of the existence of God and a sign of the apocalypse like some crackpot preacher in California (Percy, *Second Coming*, 198).

Throughout the novel, the one-eyed mountain on which he lives and on which the golf course of his pleasure lies, takes on a brooding presence, symbolizing his father and his father's suicide: "He gazed up at the round one-eyed mountain, which seemed to gaze back with an ironical expression" (Percy, *Second Coming*, 6). This ironic stance recalls Will's childhood impressions of his father's demeanor especially on the evening of his suicide. The mountain's presence looms near when Will is fingering his Luger and toying with the idea of suicide; the suggestion of death in the form of a dark bird enters the scene: "In the corner of his eye a dark bird flew through the woods, keeping pace with

him. He knew what to do" (Percy, *Second Coming*, 13).
But he does not do it. Another time while playing golf he
slices into the woods. Holding his golf club as one holds
a rifle, he climbs the fence and the stand of chestnuts
there reminds him of pin oaks and the day his father
attempted to shoot both of them. As he had that day,
again he falls down unconscious. Only this time he
awakes to Allison and her greenhouse which snuggles
against the mountain. In another incident in the story
he claims ownership of the mountain.

So it is that the mountain is the territory of his
pilgrimage. During a prenuptial party for his daughter, a
cloud settles down from the mountaintop and surges,
like Hamlet's ghost, around his house. It inspires Will
and beckons to him. Enshrouded by the fog, he begins
his journey from the golf course, a fixture of his past life:
"the golf links was like his own soul's terrain. Every
inch of it was a place where he had been before. He
knew it like a lover knows his beloved's body" (Percy,
Second Coming, 208). When "by dead reckoning he
came onto number seventeen tee..." he leaves it all
behind, straddles the fence and finds the secret entrance to the cave. "It pleased him that the great cave
should have such a banal entrance. Far below in the
valley at the proper entrance to Lost Cove Cave, an
underground river flowed into the sunlight through a
cathedral arch of stone" (Percy, *Second Coming*, 209).
He enters the mountain and becomes part of its living
innards. He crawls down, down into the cave of his
childhood, remembering each slide, crawl, and chimney
chamber. The chimney which is his destination leads to
a chamber shaped like a pod where a tiger had died
32,000 years before. Here he settles comfortably to wait
for God to show Himself. Or it will become his tomb.

Instead, thanks again to ingenious Percyan humor, he gets a toothache. For Percy, man's apocalyptic moments must ever be interrupted by the mundane. Will reacts instinctively to the pain and nausea of his malady and seeks escape. Sourwood Mountain spews him out, headfirst. Like Tom More, Will Barrett is reborn; his second coming is to an Eden and to a new Eve and a new life to make. He is certain he has found an answer, but is not yet sure what it is. Percy's new Adam is helpless as a babe at first, tended by the New Eve, Allison, also trying to make a new life and a new communication. Fascinated by the theory of language, Percy provides his two desperate and disturbed lovers coming back to a fresh life in the world a charming poetic language inspired by truth and love.

BELIEF

hen Binx Bolling returns to New Orleans with Kate after their desperate journey to Chicago, he remarks, "'The Lord of Misrule reigned yesterday'" (Percy, *Moviegoer*, 230). It will soon be Ash Wednesday and also Binx's thirtieth birthday. "Canal Street is dark and almost empty. The last parade, the Krewe of Comus, has long since disappeared down Royal Street with its shuddering floats and its blazing flambeau" (Percy, *Moviegoer*, 217-18). After the wonder of the parade, the debris must be collected.

He is in disgrace with his aunt, having run off with suicidal Kate and not told anyone where they were going. His journey has been disasterous and he is in despair. He has learned nothing. He is "now in the thirty-first year of my dark pilgrimage on this earth and knowing less than I ever knew before, having learned only to recognize merde ..." (Percy, *Moviegoer*, 228). He makes no answers to his aunt's scorching comments.

He goes home to his middle ground, Gentilly, but even that is "swept fitfully by desire and by an east wind from the burning swamps at Chef Menteur" (Percy, *Moviegoer*, 227). Everything is ashes and despair. He becomes increasingly fearful Kate will not come to him as she has promised. "A watery sunlight breaks through the smoke of the Chef and turns the sky yellow. Elysian Fields glistens like a vat of sulfur; the playground looks as if it alone had survived the end of the world" (Percy, *Moviegoer*, 231).

When Kate finally arrives "sooty-eyed and nowhere," he is able to hope. "Is it possible that ... it is not too late?" (Percy, *Moviegoer*, 231). He is able to slowly surmount his despair and his aunt's despair and Kate's despair and believe it is not yet the end of the world. Kate asks him what he plans to do and he is able to think: "There is only one thing I can do: listen to people, see how they stick themselves into the world, hand them along a ways in their dark journey and be handed along, and for good and selfish reasons" (Percy, *Moviegoer*, 233).

The final scene of the novel is typical of Percy's understated, compassionate understanding of small happenings. As he and Kate are parked in front of the church, they observe a Negro enter. Binx observes: "He is more respectable than respectable" (Percy, *Moviegoer*, 233). When he comes out again, Binx remarks:

> His forehead is an ambiguous sienna color and pied: it is impossible to be sure that he received

ashes. When he gets in his Mercury, he does not leave immediately but sits looking down at something on the seat beside him. A sample case? An insurance manual? I watch him closely in the rearview mirror. It is impossible to say why he is here. Is it part and parcel of the complex business of coming up in the world? Or is it because he believes that God himself is present here at the corner of Elysian Fields and Bons Enfants? Or is he here for both reasons: through some dim dazzling trick of grace, coming for the one and receiving the other as God's own importunate bonus?

It is impossible to say (Percy, *Moviegoer*, 234-35).

Percy's characters are not given startling revelations. Binx wryly observes: "I am a member of my mother's family after all and so naturally shy away from the subject of religion. . . ." But it is clear that Binx is hopeful enough to continue his journey and "plant a foot in the right place as the opportunity presents itself . . ." (Percy, *Moviegoer*, 237).

In the epilogue Binx and Kate are married, and his aunt settles on being fond of him as he is. Binx's half-brother Lonnie is dying and Binx is able to be of comfort to the family. Lonnie's younger brother Donice asks, "'When Our Lord raises us up on the last day will Lonnie still be in a wheelchair or will he be like us?'" It seems very important to Donice and the other children to know if Lonnie will be able then to ski. Binx takes their concern seriously and gives them the assurance they seek.

In the matter of Percy's use of symbols, one must take care not to suggest that he uses them either obviously or artificially. Never are they anything but natural to the description and the terrain. His vines are part of nature's reclamation. His golf course is a reality of the Southern good life. His one-eyed mountain is indigenous to the Carolinas, and his birds, especially the hawk, are part both of Manhattan and the Southern woods.

Percy's use of hawks merits further attention. Birds have been symbolic of the spiritual in poetry from ancient writers to the present. Percy uses the hawk in particular in this spiritual way in the two novels of Will Barrett, *The Last Gentleman* and *The Second Coming.* In *The Last Gentleman*, Will Barrett first becomes drawn to a hawk in Central Park. As he notes the bird again and again on his search and journey, its significance as the correlative of the spiritual becomes more focused. This clarity is illustrated when Will, during an attack of amnesia, happens upon Kitty's sister Val, a Catholic nun, in a setting connected to his past, the now defunct Phillips Academy in Alabama. On a hunch that he really knows the place and that he isn't having a déjà vu experience, he has driven in to explore it. Unexpectedly, he finds Val, who is feeding her pet hawk through the wire of a chicken coop. Oddly enough she seems to be expecting him and is quick to give him an important message: "'Sutter and Jamie were here. They said I was to tell you they were headed for Santa Fe'" (Percy, *Last Gentleman,* 284). "Santa Fe," of course, means *holy faith.*

> Instead of leaving, he watched her. It came to him for a second time that he didn't like her, particularly her absorption with the hawk. It was a chicken hawk with an old rusty shoulder and a black nostril.

She attended to the hawk with a buzzing antic manner which irritated him. It scandalized him slightly, like the Pope making a fuss over a canary. He was afraid she might call the hawk by some such name as Saint Blaise (Percy, *Last Gentleman*, 285).

This observation follows exactly in the abrasive vein that Will and Val have always reacted to each other, yet suggests that there is something unconsciously passing between them: a transfer of grace, of inspiration. Will talks to Val as she feeds her old and battered hawk entrails. ". . . and the hawk cocked his eye. The engineer thought about the falcon in Central Park: I could see him better at one mile than this creature face to face" (Percy, *Last Gentleman*, 289). Will himself makes the connection of the two hawks and suggests that Val's connection with this one puts him off.

As Val speaks, Will's amnesia recedes; the message was the direction he needed to continue his journey. By the time he leaves, Sister Val has extracted from Will most of his cash for the mute black children she is dedicated to teach. Sutter later tells Will that Val had come to Alabama to begin her little school and wait for a sign from God. "'There she sits in the woods as if the world had ended and she was one of the Elected Ones left to keep the Thing going, but the world has not ended . . .'" (Percy, *Last Gentleman*, 363). Sutter's analysis of his sister's vocation concludes: "'I could make some sense of her notion of being the surviving remnant to her Catholic Thing (which has to prevail, you see, in spite of all, yes, I don't mind that) set down back there in that God-forsaken place. That was fitting. But she changed, you see. *She became hopeful*'" (Percy, *Last Gentleman*, 363). Here Sutter is recalling us to the

Guardini prediction of the end of the modern world, when the love, including the love for her mute charges as she teaches them to speak, has made Val hopeful that the world will not end; and that, therefore, she must reach out to others as well.

Up to this point in the novel, young Will Barrett, the engineer, has kept himself open to the desires and whims of Jamie, who is dying. He has done no engineering in a creative sense, but only in the implementation of what Jamie has wanted to do. When he overtakes Sutter and Jamie in Santa Fe, Will finds Jamie in poor condition in the hospital. It is then that he truly becomes an engineer. Sutter is in despair and unable to help his brother.

Sutter's first words to Will are, "'Are you Philip and is this the Gaza Desert?'" (Percy, *Last Gentleman*, 345). The reference is to the apostle Philip who brought the "good news" of Christ to the eunuch in the desert. At the time, Will does not understand. Nonetheless he is unwittingly bearing that tiding from Val and it is only at the end that he realizes it. He begins by being the loving friend and companion to Jamie, playing cards with him and reading to him. "The book was the safest, sunniest most inviolate circle of all" (Percy, *Last Gentleman*, 356). But death and salvation invade the circle in a few days.

When Jamie asks Will to call Val, he does so. Val charges him to have Jamie baptized. Will agrees only to ask Jamie if he wishes to be baptized. He returns to find Jamie's condition worsened and his heart fibrillating. Will, with his new freedom and authority, demands a priest, doctors, nurses. Only then does Sutter arrive at the hospital.

In Percy's hands the episode of Jamie's death and

rebirth is unforgettable, contrasting the cold of the sick-room manipulations of the hospital staff and the warmth of the love which flows between brothers and friends. The novelist conveys with great skill the salvific interplay between the acceptance of faith by Jamie and the unconscious reception of faith by Will.

The priest is an athletic robot, at first reluctant to have any part of the situation but overwhelmed by Will's strength. Since Sutter, sunk in his own egocentric despair, has no objection, he prepares to baptize the unconscious patient "conditionally." The priest senses Will's role as engineer and names him the friend "who loves" the dying youth.

Percy's knowledge of medicine and the machinations of dying heighten not only the tensions of the terrible event, but the mystery of what happens. The passage is perhaps Percy's most powerful in its balance of irony and spiritual presence. Jamie regains consciousness, and, after an extreme effort to attend to the purging of his body, collapses again into a state where only Will, the medium, can interpret to the priest Jamie's questions and answers. Will's acute awareness of all the persons in the drama includes Sutter, the brother who can only perform as physician: "Sutter conducted Jamie back to bed fondly and even risibly. Suddenly the engineer remembered that this was the way Negro servants handle the dying, as if it were the oldest joke of all" (Percy, *Last Gentleman*, 386).

In his role as interpreter, Will also becomes an instrument of grace. Percy observes: "The engineer, who did not know how he knew, was not even sure he had heard Jamie or had tuned him in in some other fashion . . ." (Percy, *Last Gentleman*, 390). When Jamie asks, through Will, why he should believe the truths the priest has outlined to him, the priest replies simply and surely, "'If it were not true, . . . then I would not be here. That is why I am here to tell you'" (Percy, *Last Gentleman*, 388). The youth accepts the priest's apostolic authority. The robot has become the conduit of grace. As Jamie nods his acceptance to the engineer, the priest baptizes him and Jamie clings to his hand. Will, the engineer and conductor, is also a participant in the miracle of belief.

Three brief pages complete the novel but they are fraught with meaning for both Will and Sutter. Will runs after Sutter, who is fleeing. He calls for him to wait, and asks him a question to detain him: "'What happened back there?'" Sutter's reply is impatient, "'Do you have to know what I think before you know what you think?'" (Percy, *Last Gentleman*, 391). Only then does Will realize that this is no longer true—he has caught what Sutter has missed. His response is immediate and positive. He must do something to deter Sutter from his suicidal bent. The priest has correctly named Will "the friend who loves you," and he transfers his concern to Sutter. Will persists, "'Dr. Vaught, I need you. I, Will Barrett . . .'" (Percy, *Last Gentleman*, 393). With this, Percy indicates Will's breakthrough to life and love. He quotes Romano Guardini's *The End of the Modern World* in the beginning of the book: "Love will disappear from the face of the public world, but the more precious will be that love which flows from one lonely person to another . . ." (Guardini, *End*, 132). The quotation's meaning is illustrated in Will's ability to reach out to Sutter and acknowledge his responsibility. He sprints after Sutter's Edsel, which has again begun to move:

> "Wait," he shouted in a dead run. The Edsel paused, sighed, and stopped.

Strength flowed like oil into his muscles and he ran with great joyous ten-foot antelope bounds.

The Edsel waited for him. (Percy, *Last Gentleman*, 393).

Percy has told us that another time Will had called "wait" three times—to his father before he shot himself to death. Then, his father had not waited. This time the engineer has won one for life.

Thomas More, the "bad Catholic" of *Love in the Ruins*, states again and again he has not lost his faith: He acknowledges that he is "bad" because he does not go to church and lives in sin. Yet he cannot deny God or Christ and the truth of Catholic doctrine. He expresses it this way:

I, for example, am a Roman Catholic, albeit a bad one. I believe in the Holy Catholic Apostolic and Roman Church, in God the Father, in the election of the Jews, in Jesus Christ His Son our Lord, who founded the Church on Peter his first vicar, which will last until the end of the world. Some years ago, however, I stopped eating Christ in Communion, stopped going to mass, and have since fallen into a disorderly life. I believe in God and the whole business but I love women best, music and science next, whiskey next, God fourth, and my fellowman hardly at all. Generally I do as I please. A man, wrote John, who says he believes in God and does not keep his commandments is a liar. If John is right, then I am a liar. Nevertheless, I still believe (Percy, *Love*, 6).

Thus does Thomas More, descendent of St. Thomas More who died for his faith, present his dilemma. No, he has not lost his faith among his scientific pursuits, but he has lost his hope amidst the tragedies of his life: loss of wife and child and the longing and ambitions he gives effort to. He lives in a house in Paradise Estates and only when he leaves it forever does he find himself.

Tom's loss of hope and his irreligious tendencies disturbed his young daughter before she died. Tom recalls the conversation in which he confesses his lapse and the child's concern for his spiritual health. Her answer is simple yet certain, remembered from the catechism class. Tom tells it thus:

> "Papa, have you lost your faith?"
> "No."
> Samantha asked me the question as I stood by her bed. The neuroblastoma had pushed one eye out and around the nosebridge so she looked like a Picasso profile.
> "Then why don't you go to mass any more?"
> "I don't know. Maybe because you don't go with me."
> "Papa, you're in greater danger than Mama."
> "How is that?"
> "Because she is protected by Invincible Ignorance."
> "That's true," I said, laughing.
> "She doesn't know any better."
> "She doesn't."
> "You do."
> "Yes."
> "Just promise me one thing, Papa."
> "What's that?"

"Don't commit the one sin for which there is no forgiveness."

"Which one is that?"

"The sin against grace. If God gives you the grace to believe in him and love him and you refuse, the sin will not be forgiven you."

"I know." I took her hand, which even then still looked soiled and chalk-dusted like a schoolgirl's (Percy, *Love,* 373-74).

Here we see Tom confronted by the pain of someone he loves dearly and his inability as a doctor to do anything about it or to prevent her death. Because he cannot solve the problem of pain and the inevitability of death, life loses all meaning. He seeks an answer in science and dismisses the spiritual explanation completely. He renews his efforts to restore mankind to a primal Eden through his invention. With another breakthrough he hopes to cure the ills of man in addition to diagnosing them. He does not see that even Adam had longings beyond Paradise.

When his young swamp friend describes to Tom a life where he could live "completely and in the moment the way a prothonotary warbler lives flashing holy fire," Tom begins to realize that he cannot ignore the spiritual side of man (Percy, *Love,* 368). Samantha's deathbed perception born of her catechism recitation must be accepted if he truly believes. If he believes, he must try to practice.

The climax is precipitated by Art Immelmann's demand that he and Ellen, his innocent and true love, come with him to Denmark. Tom realizes that his sin in submitting to the devil must not involve Ellen, and that while he lives he can still save himself as well. Percy details the exchange in this way:

> Slinging the device from his shoulder, he holds out both hands. "The two of you will come with me."
>
> "We have to go," whispers Ellen, shrinking against me.
>
> "No we don't."
>
> "If we both go, Chief, maybe it will be all right."
>
> "No it won't," I say, not taking my eyes from Art, whose arms are outstretched like the Christ at Sacre Coeur in New Orleans.
>
> "We'll be happy in Copenhagen," murmurs Art....
>
> .... What is frightening is his smiling assurance. He doesn't even need the lapsometer! (Percy, *Love*, 376).

Tom thus is shocked back into hope and humility and aware now that his lapsometer really can't cure; he begins to pray for the first time in years: "'Sir Thomas More, kinsman, saint, best dearest merriest of Englishmen, pray for us and drive this son of a bitch hence'" (Percy, *Love*, 376). The devil vanishes into smoke. In the epilogue Tom makes his confession, makes public his faith, and reaches out to others in the community of faith.

In *Lancelot*, Lance's one-sided conversations are often a tirade against his priest-psychiatrist's Catholicism. He scorns the Church's inability to prevent the modern breakdown in morals. His cynical interpretation of his friend's motivation in going to Africa to serve and his current plans for a center in Alabama are reminiscent of Sutter's analysis of Sister Val's motives in her Tyree school in *The Last Gentleman*. Both Lancelot and Sutter are akin in the stage of despair which they have reached, except that Sutter's violence is turned inward while Lance's is turned toward others. Lance speculates: "'I might have tolerated you and your Catholic Church, and even joined it, if you had remained true to yourself. Now you're part of the age'" (Percy, *Lancelot,* 157).

As he progresses, one of the first things Lance rejects is violence, indicating that only "crazies" have recourse to it. Yet when he leaves the hospital he still plans to carry with him his bowie knife, with which he has done great violence in the past. He declares: "We shall start a new order of things" (Percy, *Lancelot*, 156). He rants about the new age he will help create which will be based:

> ... on that stern rectitude valued by the new breed and marked by the violence which will attend its breech.... Don't speak to me of Christian love. Whatever came of it? I'll tell you what came of it. It got mouthed off on the radio and TV from the pulpit and that was the end of it. The Jews knew better. Billy Graham lay down with Nixon and got up with a different set of fleas, but the Jewish prophets lived in deserts and wildernesses and had no part with corrupt kings (Percy, *Lancelot,* 158).

The dark knight becomes less and less sneering as he makes his way back to sanity. As he ruminates on the moral plight of the deep South and "the great dying cities of the North," he announces his choice of Virginia as the place to begin his new life, with Anna, the girl in the next room, "the new Adam and Eve of the new world" (Percy, *Lancelot*, 251).

Armed with plans for a new Eden and his bowie knife, Lancelot has his last conversation with Percival. He suddenly makes a confession:

> Yes, I'm quite all right now. No, no confession forthcoming, Father, as you well know. But there is one thing.... There is a coldness.... You know the feeling of numbness and coldness, no, not a feeling, but a lack of feeling, that I spoke of during the events at Belle Isle? I told you it might have been the effect of the hurricane, the low pressure, methane, whatever. But I still feel it....
>
> I feel so cold, Percival. Tell me the truth. Is everyone cold now or is it only I?
>
> What? You remind me that I said in the beginning that there was something I wanted to ask you.... The question is: Why did I discover nothing at the heart of the evil? There was no "secret" after all, no discovery, no flickering of interest, nothing at all, not even any evil.... There is no unholy grail just as there was no Holy Grail (Percy, *Lancelot*, 253).

Then Percy has Lancelot, empty and cold, turn toward the only friend, the only person he can talk to, and ask his first question: "'You gaze at me with such— what? Sadness? Love? What about love? Do I think I can ever love anyone?'" (Percy, *Lancelot*, 254). The priest's name in religion—John, the beloved disciple of Jesus— becomes significant. And now, feeling love again for the first time, Lancelot is moved to say: "'You know, something has changed in you. I have the feeling that while I was talking and changing, you were listening and changing.... You're waiting for me to finish" (Percy, *Lancelot,* 254). And Lancelot's plan, as he then enumerates it, now includes the possibility of God's existence.

In the remarkable exchange that follows, Lancelot becomes more and more open as the priest becomes more and more affirmative in his own belief. When Lancelot finishes, he leaves the door open: "'Is there anything you wish to tell me before I leave?'" (Percy, *Lancelot*, 257). As John answers in the affirmative, his only recorded words in the entire novel, Lancelot is finally ready to listen. The reader is faced with the possibility that the priest has the "good news" and Lancelot is open for the first time to hear it.

*T**he Second Coming* implies a second coming of Christ and a new beginning for Will, the aging protagonist of the story. He has decried the Jews' departure from his South, the unheeding and prevalent Christianity there which has lost Christ. Will entered the mountain in one last desperate reach for a reason to exist. He becomes the "mole" he calls his father, but the tomb he has chosen is a womb which expells him to a new birth, his own second coming. The sign he seeks of God's existence reveals itself slowly, growing with his and Allison's love.

Percy again presents the paradox of true sanity: Allison is slowly emerging from her "Sirius dwarf star" state after fleeing shock therapy in a mental home; Will has been diagnosed as having a serious chemical imbalance which affects his brain to the point of suicide. Yet he is the one person she can expertly administer to in his unconscious state, and later communicate with as he awakens in her new Eden greenhouse, symbol of new birth. The new, alliterative and rhyming language they develop for this love communication is suggestive of Adam and Eve's first efforts at language. Both are able to reenter the outside world; they make new plans with other lost souls in the home for the aging.

The last episode of the novel, a dialog between Will and old Father Weatherbee, demonstrates Percy's ability to present the interplay of physical reality and spiritual being. The curious old priest is frightened by Will's newfound life and the persistence of his search for belief. When asked to perform the marriage of Will and Allie, he only wishes to turn Will over to Father Curl. Will tells him, "'No, you're my man. I perceive that you seem to know something—and that by the same token Jack Curl does not'" (Percy, *Second Coming*, 358). Trapped, the little old priest "craned up his neck like a Philippine bird and looked in every direction except Will Barrett's. 'How can we be the best dearest most generous people on earth, and at the same time so unhappy?'" (Percy, *Second Coming*, 359). The old missionary continues:

There is a tiny village in Mindanao near Naga-Naga on the coast, which I was able to visit only once a year. They are as poor as any people on earth, yet how kind and gentle and loving they are to each other! And happy! When I would come to the village little children would run out laughing with joy to see me, take me by the hand, and lead me around the village to visit the old and the sick and the blind—and they were even happier to see me than the children! They believed me! They believed the Gospel whole and entire, and the teachings of the church. They said that if I told them, then it must be true or I would not have gone to so much trouble . . .

. . . "Right!" cried Will Barrett. In his excitement he had risen from his chair and started around the desk. "Tell me something, Father. Do you believe that Christ will come again and that in fact there are certain unmistakable signs of his coming in these very times?" (Percy, *Second Coming*, 359-60).

Will does not get a direct answer from the old priest. Will has startled him. "The bad eye spun and the good eye looked back at him . . . the old man did not move but looked at him with a new odd expression." Will thinks of Allison:

What is it I want from her and him, he wondered, not only want but must have? Is she a gift and therefore a sign of a giver? Could it be that the Lord is here, masquerading behind this simple silly holy face? Am I crazy to want both, her and Him? No, not want, must have. And will have (Percy, *Second Coming,* 360).

Will has found answer enough to keep him searching, and the answer brings to mind again the Guardini observations about the new era after the end of the modern world—an era of struggle and hope and above all, love.

THE MACULATE CHRIST

he crumbling end of the modern world of Walker Percy is most vivid in the third novel, *Love in the Ruins*, set in the near future when decay is rampant, making contrasts more apparent.

The sprouting and resurgence of uncontrollable vines in the South has always been a sign of decline. When the old structures and the land were left untended, wisteria, trumpet, and a thousand other wild vines took over. Thus it is in *Love in the Ruins*. The overgrowth invades even the sacred country club. A tendril has sprouted through the wormy cypress of the club bar and twined around a bottle of Southern Comfort. The Pro Shop is deserted and overgrown with vines; the club pool is green with algae; broken concrete is filled in everywhere with green. No one notices but Dr. More.

The open back door of his office presents Tom More with a constant reminder:

> The asphalt of the empty plaza still bubbles under the hot July sun. Through the shimmer of heat one can see the broken storefronts beyond the plaza. A green line wavers in midair over the pavement, like the hanging gardens of Babylon. It is not a mirage, however. I know what it is. A green growth has taken root on the flat roofs of the stores (Percy, *Love*, 23).

Walker Percy makes this description all the more ominous with the use of the term "green line," signifying a military formation drawn up in battle: nature itself is warring against the crumbling civilization. The reference to Babylon illustrates the decadence and opulence which led to the fall of that civilization.

In *Love in the Ruins*, although Tom More has not lost his faith completely, he has lost the practice of it in his despair over the death of his daughter. Before she died, Samantha, in childlike simplicity, worried that he had given up going to Mass and warned him, "'If God gives you the grace to believe in him and love him and you refuse, the sin will not be forgiven you'" (Percy, *Love*, 374). What Tom rejects is the acceptance of pain and suffering that goes along with his faith. Even his lapsometer is based on a desire to rid humanity of the effects of original sin, and return the Earth to Eden before the fall. However, he is forced repeatedly to face his own failure to do so or to help anyone else to any degree. At one point in the novel, in despair, he sees himself in the bar mirror:

> In the dark mirror there is a dim hollow-eyed Spanish Christ. The pox is spreading on his face. Va-

cuoles are opening in his chest. It is the new Christ, the spotted Christ, the maculate Christ, the sinful Christ. The old Christ died for our sins and it didn't work, we were not reconciled. The new Christ shall reconcile man with his sins (Percy, *Love*, 153).

What Percy is illustrating here is Christ's admonitions in the Gospel of the Last Judgment to seek Him in others, even the least, the most sinful. How shall man be reconciled in Percy's future? Through the same way Guardini predicted for the torn future—a reconciliation through love: "Love will disappear from the face of the public world, but the more precious will be that love which flows from one lonely person to another ... (Guardini, *End*, 132).

Percy continues his illustration of his "maculate Christ":

The new Christ lies drunk in a ditch. Victor Charles and Leroy Ledbetter pass by and see him. "Victor, do you love me?" "Sho, Doc." "Leroy, do you love me?" "Cut it out, Tom, you know better than to ask that." "Then y'all help me." "O.K., Doc." They laugh and pick up the new Christ, making a fireman's carry, joining four hands. They love the new Christ and so they love each other (Percy, *Love*, 153).

In this passage the segregationist and the black, both Tom's friends, are reconciled and labor together. In each of the five novels Percy leaps from faith to that love which is to save the future and which is to remake a new world from the torn remnants of the old. This compassion is Walker Percy's solution for a new era. His compassion is a remarkable quality, rarely found in modern writers. This compassion is a quality of love which enlightens his hapless characters. Binx Bolling's primary concern becomes Kate; the young Will Barrett's, Jamie; Lancelot in his renewal turns to Percival; Tom More reaches out to Ellen, and the older Will Barrett rediscovers love in Allison. The same largess is found not only in Percy's protagonists but also in his attitude toward all his characters.

British novelist Graham Greene is another modern writer who accomplishes this remarkable compassion in his fictions. It is most apparent in *The Honorary Consul, The End of the Affair, The Heart of the Matter, The Human Factor* and *Monsignor Quixote*. Greene's satire is warmed by it. Enemies are reconciled through it. In his latest fiction, *Monsignor Quixote*, Greene has paired two natural antagonists, the simple old-fashioned parish priest and the atheistic Communist mayor of the town. Compassion has made them friends and travelling companions. At the end, love is Monsignor Quixote's legacy to his friend. A passage which projects this idea is the last:

> The Mayor didn't speak again before they reached Orense; an idea quite strange to him had lodged in his brain. Why is it that the hate of a man—even a man like Franco—dies with his death, and yet love, the love which he had begun to feel for Father Quixote, seemed now to live and grow in spite of the final separation and the final silence—for how long, he wondered with a kind of fear, was it possible for that love of his to continue? And to what end? (Graham Greene, *Monsignor Quixote* [New York: Simon and Schuster, 1982] 221).

Greene seems to imply that the Mayor, descendent of the original Don Quixote's Sancho, has been infected with the compassion and love left him by Monsignor Quixote, and that he, too, must pass it on. There again sounds the echo of Guardini's "love which flows from one lonely person to another...." Yet neither Greene nor Percy can be accused of being anything but realists, nor of presenting other than as a human being, the "maculate Christ."

The sprouting of the vines in *Love in the Ruins* can also be interpreted as one of Percy's paradoxes. Along with decay, the growth also stands for the resurgence of Nature, of life, of hope. With the blotting out of the corruptible creations of man, there will be new beginnings with the miraculous sprouting of organic life. For man, after Ash Wednesday's ashes, comes the new life of Easter. A return to basic values and love is at the heart of Walker Percy's hope for the future. His novel of the future ends with the beginning of Christmas Day: "... and the Lord is here, a holy night and surely that is all one needs." Tom More and his wife go to bed "twined about each other as the ivy twineth ... (Percy, *Love*, 403). This triad of belief, hope, and love is Walker Percy's legacy to the future of the postmodern world.

BIBLIOGRAPHY

Broughton, Panthea Reid, ed. *The Art of Walker Percy: Stratagems for Being*. Baton Rouge and London: Louisiana State Univ. Press, 1979.

Coles, Robert. *Walker Percy: An American Search*. Boston: Little, Brown and Company, 1978.

Fuller, R. Buckminster. *Critical Path*. New York: St. Martin's Press, 1981.

Greene, Graham. *Monsignor Quixote*. New York: Simon and Schuster, 1982.

Guardini, Romano. *The End of the Modern World: A Search for Orientation*. Trans. Joseph Theman and Herbert Burke. New York: Sheed and Ward, 1956.

Hobson, Linda Whitney. "The Study of Consciousness: An Interview with Walker Percy." *Georgia Review*, 35 (1981): 50-60.

Luschei, Martin. *The Sovereign Wayfarer: Walker Percy's Diagnosis of the Malaise*. Baton Rouge: Louisiana State Univ. Press, 1972.

Mississippi Writers Talking. Vol. 2. Interviews with Walker Percy, Ellen Douglas, Willie Morris, Margaret Walker Alexander, James Whitehead, Turner Cassidy. Interviewed by John Griffin Jones. Jackson: Univ. Press of Mississippi, 1983.

Percy, Walker. *Lancelot*. New York: Farrar, Straus and Giroux, 1977.

Percy, Walker. *The Last Gentleman*. New York: Farrar, Straus and Giroux, 1966.

Percy, Walker. *Lost in the Cosmos: The Last Self-Help Book*. New York: Farrar, Straus and Giroux, 1983.

Percy, Walker. *Love in the Ruins: The Adventures of a Bad Catholic at a Time near the End of the World*. New York: Farrar, Straus and Giroux, 1971.

Percy, Walker. *The Message in the Bottle: How Queer Man Is, How Queer Language Is, and What One Has to Do with the Other*. New York: Farrar, Straus and Giroux, 1975.

Percy, Walker. *The Moviegoer*. New York: Alfred A. Knopf, 1961.

Percy, Walker. *The Second Coming*. New York: Farrar, Straus and Giroux, 1980.

Teilhard de Chardin, Pierre. *The Phenomenon of Man*. Introd. Sir Julian Huxley. New York and Evanston: Harper and Row, 1959.

Tharpe, Jac. *Walker Percy*. Boston: Twayne Publishers, 1983.

Tharpe, Jac, ed. *Walker Percy: Art and Ethics*. Jackson: Univ. Press of Mississippi, 1980.

INDEX